C0-EEU-302

About the Book

California's history—from the first coastal explorations by Juan Rodríguez Cabrillo to the thirty-one-gun salute celebrating the state's entry into the Union—is seen through the fascinating firsthand accounts of explorers, missionaries, adventurers, and settlers.

The extraordinarily wide range of source material selected by George Sanderlin includes records of early attempts to convert the Indians, Nikolai Rezanov's letters to the Russian-American Company outlining his bold plans for the Russian takeover of California, James O. Pattie's account of his experiences crossing the Colorado Desert, personal letters describing Louise Amelia Clappe's life in a gold mining town, and many many others.

Their compelling stories are fully integrated by George Sanderlin's strong narrative to provide an exciting, vivid understanding of the people, the land, and the events that marked the settlement of California.

THE SETTLEMENT OF CALIFORNIA

by George Sanderlin

Coward, McCann & Geoghegan, Inc.
New York

Jacket: A mid-seventeenth-century map shows the popular misconception of California as an island.

Courtesy of Title Insurance and Trust Company

Copyright © 1972 by George Sanderlin

All rights reserved. This book, or parts thereof, may not be reproduced in any form without permission in writing from the publishers. Published simultaneously in Canada by Longmans Canada Limited, Toronto.

SBN: GB–698–30456–X
SBN: TR–698–20190–6

Library of Congress Catalog Card Number: 72-76697

Printed in the United States of America

12 up

The author gratefully acknowledges permission to reprint the following:

Reprinted by permission of Coward, McCann & Geoghegan, Inc. from *The Course of Empire: First Hand Accounts of California in the Days of the Gold Rush of '49* compiled by Valeska Bari. Copyright 1931 by Valeska Bari.

From *Anza's California Expeditions*, by Herbert Eugene Bolton. Originally published by the University of California Press; reprinted by permission of The Regents of the University of California.

Adapted from Herbert Bolton: *Spanish Exploration in the Southwest*, Barnes & Noble Books, New York, New York.

From *History of California: The Spanish Period*, by Charles E. Chapman. Copyright 1921 by The Macmillan Company, renewed 1949 by Aimee F. Chapman. Reprinted by permission of The Macmillan Company.

From *The Cruise of the Portsmouth*, by Joseph T. Downey, edited by Howard Lamar. Copyright 1958 by Yale University Library. Published by Yale University Press, and reprinted with its permission.

From *The Poetry of Robert Frost*, by Robert Frost, edited by Edward Connery Lathem. Copyright 1969 by Holt, Rinehart and Winston, Inc. Published by Holt, Rinehart and Winston, Inc. and reprinted with its permission.

From *Palou's Life of Fray Junipero Serre*, translated by Maynard J. Geiger, O.F.M., Washington, D.C. 1955. Copyright 1955 by Academy of American Franciscan History. Reprinted by permission of the Academy of American Franciscan History.

From *The Russian-American Company*, by S. B. Okun, translated by Carl Ginsburg. Copyright 1951 by the American Council of Learned Societies. Published by Harvard University Press and reprinted with its permission.

From *Chronicles of the Gringos*, by George Winston Smith and Charles Judah. Copyright 1968 by the University of New Mexico Press and reprinted with its permission.

From *Juan Rodriguez Cabrillo*, by Henry R. Wagner. Copyright 1941 by California Historical Society. Reprinted by permission of California Historical Society.

To my wife

Contents

Prologue   11

    1   Discoverers from Castile   17
    2   Father Serra and the Missions   49
    3   The Russian Bear   79
    4   Boston Clippers and Mountain Men   101
    5   The Stars and Stripes   131
    6   "Gold! Gold! Gold from the American River!"   161
    7   The Thirty-first State   207

Epilogue   215
A Table of Events   218
Books About the History of California   220
Index   221

Early explorers thought California was an island.

Prologue

An eerie wind springs up. There is a low, rumbling roar accompanied by a surging rolling motion of the ground, then a thunderous crash of rocks, shattering and upheaval of the earth's crust. . . .

Thus, eons ago, California was born. A series of titanic earthquakes lifted its scarred young mountains high above the Pacific. They shaped a land that was to have an exciting and romantic history.

The California we know is a great slab of the Pacific coast. To make a "California" in the East, you would have to rub out the boundaries of all the states bordering the Atlantic, from Maryland through Georgia, and join these states together.

California also resembles an enlarged, economy-size Portugal. Like Portugal, it runs north and south and occupies the southwest portion of a continent. Like Portugal, too, it faces a mighty ocean which is becoming a crossroads of nations—just as the Atlantic, which the Portuguese called the "Green Sea of Darkness," did four centuries ago. However, California's length (824 miles) and width (252 miles) give it an area larger than that of Norway or the British Isles.

California is shaped like an oblong coffee scoop, but without the open end. The mountain chains which make up its long sides—the Coast Range and the Sierra Nevada

—close at both ends. The 400-mile-long Central Valley is the trough of the scoop, between the two high sides.

Europeans arriving by sea stared at the jumble of peaks, valleys, and canyons that make up the Coast Range. They scanned the broad sands in the south and the narrow gravel beaches and cliffs of the north for a break, a harbor. At first the Spaniards found only San Diego Bay, which curves back south like a fishhook from its entry at Point Loma. Later, journeying overland, they stumbled upon the great inland sea which is San Francisco Bay; it is 50 miles long and is connected to the Pacific by a fog-hung strait, the Golden Gate.

Between the Coast Range and the Pacific there is a narrow corridor, just wide enough to become a much-traveled road between these two ports. Along this King's Highway were strung the red-tiled adobe missions of the Franciscans. Fronting it were the great cattle ranches, Spanish land grants of thousands of acres, reaching back into the brown hills. The spurs and ridges of the Coast Range, produced by the tremendous earthquakes, point in all directions, like jackstraws. But in this range the bold Tehachapi Mountains, at right angles to the Pacific, form a marked barrier between the dry south and the well-watered north.

For many decades the Spaniards did not venture far from the coast. When they did make their way through the Coast Range, they reached the Central Valley. The Central Valley, 400 miles long by 50 miles wide, is the heartland of California. Much of it is treeless, much of it level as a basement. It is ideal farmland, watered by the Sacramento River at its northern end and by the San Joaquin at its southern. Summers are hotter here than on the coast, winters cooler, but overall the climate is mild and the sunshine abundant. With the help of irrigation canals from the two rivers, its rich loams yield bumper crops through three growing seasons—an incredible 250 days. Fields of cotton, wheat, lettuce, and asparagus stretch as far as the eye can reach. But if your eyes tire of the green, you can lift them up to the hills—to the purple mountains that rim this enormous California garden.

The far side of California is formed by the Sierra Nevada. This is a true rampart, whose outer, eastern slope plunges down precipitously. Majestic peaks, twelve of them above 14,000 feet, stand in line, guarding the land, like a file of giants from *Gulliver's Travels*. This mountain wall stretches over 400 miles, from Mount Shasta in the north to Death Valley, 282 feet below sea level, in the south. Here is Mount Whitney, at 14,496 feet the highest mountain in the United States outside Alaska. Here are the great pines, the "Big Trees," 300 feet tall and ten centuries old, the equal of the redwoods of the Coast Range. Here the short-tempered grizzly bear once foraged, and gold glinted at the bottom of turbulent streams.

During the winter the Sierra Nevada ("The Snowy Range") lives up to its name. Fifteen-foot drifts block its passes and fill its canyons. Ages ago, slow-moving glaciers carved out its blue lakes and deep valley floors. Its finest valley is Yosemite, 4,000 feet above sea level and completely enclosed by mile-high mountains; it is like the nave of a Gothic cathedral from which the roof has been removed.

California is air-conditioned—or, rather, water-cooled. The coast from San Francisco to the Mexican border has the only truly temperate climate on the North American continent. This is owing to the presence of that great reservoir the Pacific. Temperatures over oceans vary less than those over landmasses. Prevailing westerly winds extend the moderating influence of the Pacific far inland and give California a "short" thermometer—that is, comparatively high in winter, comparatively low in summer. For example, San Diego, in the same latitude as Vicksburg, Mississippi, has a much lower average summer temperature. Towns on the Oregon border are warmer in winter than Washington, D.C., which lies much farther south.

But California has more than one climate. Its northeastern corner lies in a belt of heavy rainfall, from 65 to 110 inches per year. The Colorado Desert, on the other hand, has less than 1 inch per year, with temperatures rising to 130° in summer.

There are other aspects of California geography which are uncomfortable. Earthquake tremors rattle windows and jar the Californian out of his complaceny, reminding him of the destruction of San Francisco by quake and fire in 1906. The 1,000-mile San Andreas Fault, largest in the world, runs through South San Francisco and only 33 miles from downtown Los Angeles; more than sixty persons died in the Los Angeles earthquake of 1971, which was *not* considered a major one. At the end of the dry season, late summer brush fires, blown into raging fire storms by the east wind, threaten the bright-colored homes and char the land. Then winter rains gouge runoffs in soil stripped of its green cover and cause mudslides which bury roads and buildings. California's sunny pastoral appearance can be deceiving.

California is a rich land. Not just in gold—so much of which has now been extracted—but in many other things useful to man. For centuries it provided the red man with a balanced ecology that supported the densest Indian population in what is now the United States. It grew coarse grass for the Spaniards' cattle, wheat for the forty-niners' bread, and lumber for a later generation's redwood houses. In its soil flourished vineyards, orange groves, avocado groves, all the specialty crops for which California is now known. In the twentieth century it surprised everyone by producing a million barrels of oil a day; black derricks dotted the once-isolated coast and offshore waters.

Land of wealth, land of contrasts, land of mystery—

this is the California that the Spaniards named after the earthly paradise in a novel. This is the California which has drawn people from the four corners of the earth.

Their history is a pageant. First come the Indians, short, sturdy, brown-skinned emigrants from Asia by way of the Bering Strait. Gray-robed Franciscans follow, also *señoritas* in scarlet gowns and *caballeros* in bright-green jackets with large silver buttons. Fur-hatted Russians pursue the sea otter in San Francisco Bay. Spectacled Yankee traders bargain with Spanish rancheros for hides, and leather-shirted Yankee mountain men explore the backcountry. Forty-niners in black felt hats, blue shirts, and hip boots shoulder shovel and pick and climb down the deep, sunless gorges of the mining country, Mark Twain country, behind San Francisco.

What do they seek under the blue skies? What do they find? In the following pages we can watch them arrive in flimsy, undecked ships, on foot or on horseback, across mountain and desert. We can watch them occupy the coast and valleys, watch them mold the land and be molded by it. We can see their hopes and dreams realized or shattered.

This is their story—the story of a quest, for food, for empire, for riches, for the "good life." This is the pageant of the settlement of California.

1
Discoverers from Castile

A great island and 30 small islands which seem to be the new islands of California, rich in pearls.
—RICHARD HAKLUYT,
The Principal Navigations

Juan Rodríguez Cabrillo

Sir Frances Drake

ISLAND OF AMAZONS

Have you ever thought of California as an island? Did you know that its skies were once supposed to be full not of airplanes but of winged "griffins"—creatures that were half eagle and half lion? Griffins might snatch a man from the earth and carry him straight up, then drop him to his death! And there were no freeways—the land was paved instead with pearls and gold. . . .

This California existed only in a story, written by the Spaniard Ordóñez de Montalvo. Montalvo invented the name and the place for his novel *Las Sergas de Esplandián*. He wrote it around 1500, not long after Columbus had discovered America.

This Spanish storyteller imagined a country that belonged to ebony-colored women—women warriors who fought with bow and spear and were called "Amazons." No men were permitted in their land, a kind of "earthly paradise" of beautiful groves, rivers, gold, and gems. The story was popular, because people had been seeking the earthly paradise ever since Adam and Eve were driven from the Garden of Eden. Also, people had read about the Amazons in the works of many authors, beginning with the ancient Greek historian Herodotus.

Herodotus thought the Amazons lived on the shores of the Black Sea, but no one could find them there. Then Columbus heard reports, on his return voyage, of an island of Amazons in the Caribbean. (Later some Spaniards thought they saw Amazons beside a great river in South America and gave the river that name.)

Perhaps Ordóñez de Montalvo heard of Columbus' Caribbean Amazons and borrowed them for his novel, because he does locate their island "at the right hand of the [newly found] Indies"—that is, among the islands discovered by Columbus. In his story, he makes Calafía, the Queen of the Amazons, bring her warlike ladies from California to Constantinople. Constantinople was considered nearby because Columbus told everyone that he had reached Asia, near India. (That is why he called the red men he found "Indians.")

Queen Calafía and her Amazons helped some pagans besiege Christian Constantinople, but in the end the queen and her followers were converted and changed sides. Calafía then gave her delightful island to the Christians. Later a good many Christians—Spaniards, Englishmen, Russians, and Americans—were to try to claim the real California, named from this realm of romance.

The following passage, describing the mythical California, is from Ordóñez de Montalvo's *Las Sergas de Esplandian* (from Charles E. Chapman, *A History of California: The Spanish Period*).

Know ye that at the right hand of the Indies there is an island named California, very close to that part of the Terrestrial Paradise, which was inhabited by black women, without a single man among them, and they lived in the manner of Amazons. They were robust of body, with strong and passionate hearts and great virtues.

The island itself is one of the wildest in the world on account of the bold and craggy rocks. Their weapons were all made of gold. The island everywhere abounds with gold and precious stones, and upon it no other metal was found. They lived in caves, well excavated. They had many ships with which they sailed to other coasts to make forays, and the men whom they took as prisoners they killed. In this island, named California, there are many griffins. In no other part of the world can they be found.

And there ruled over that island of California a queen of majestic proportions, more beautiful than all others, and in the very vigor of her womanhood. She was desirous of accomplishing great deeds. She was valiant and courageous, and ardent, with a brave heart, and had ambitions to execute nobler actions than had been performed by any other ruler.

AN EPIC VOYAGE

The Caribbean islands which Christopher Columbus discovered in 1492 were stepping-stones to the mainland of the Americas. In 1519 the conquistador Hernando Cortés took a giant step west and landed on Mexico. After he overthrew the Aztec King Montezuma and seized his treasure, Cortés founded towns on Mexico's Pacific coast. Then he looked north.

What secrets were hidden behind those towering white clouds? Was more treasure like Montezuma's gold and silver concealed in some misty valley there? Did the isle of the dusky Amazons rise out of a northern sea? Or did the broad "Strait of Anian," rumored to flow west from the Atlantic, rush into the Pacific only a short way up the coast?

As fast as he could enlist conquistadors and build vessels in Mexico's Pacific ports, Cortés launched his northern expeditions. In 1533, Fortún Jiménez discovered Mexico's long northwestern peninsula and may have been the one to name it California—perhaps because pearls were found there. In 1535, Cortés himself founded a short-lived colony at La Paz, in Lower California. In 1539, he sent Francisco de Ulloa up the Gulf of California to the mouth of the Colorado River.

In 1540, Antonio de Mendoza, viceroy of New Spain (Mexico), sent out a famous land expedition under Francisco Vázquez de Coronado to hunt for the legendary Seven Cities of Cíbola. They were said to be somewhere in the Southwest. Coronado and his lieutenants found no rich cities, but they reached Kansas, discovered the Grand Canyon, and ascended the Colorado River, perhaps far enough to view Upper California—the future American state—from the east.

Finally, in 1542, Viceroy Mendoza began a two-pronged advance into the unknown. From Navidad, on the west coast of Mexico, he ordered one fleet across the Pacific to name and take formal possession of the Philippines (so-called after Prince Philip, future King of Spain). From the same port he sent another "fleet" directly north to explore the unmapped coast. This fleet consisted of two small ships which did not even have decked-over quarters for the crews.

These ships, the *San Salvador* and the *Victoria*, were commanded by a brave Portuguese captain and skillful navigator, Juan Rodríguez Cabrillo. Perhaps seeking the mysterious Strait of Anian, Cabrillo sailed with great daring into the stormy North Pacific. He inspired his nondescript crew of conscripts and natives with his own courage.

Many of his men developed scurvy, a disease caused by the lack of fresh fruits and vegetables. The consequent vitamin deficiency made the men's gums decay and their teeth fall out, caused hunger and death. Cabrillo also suffered from a food shortage, the excruciating pain of a broken arm improperly set, heavy seas and never-ending gales. He himself would not return; but his flimsy ships

would sail all the way to Oregon, and he would gain lasting fame as the discoverer of California.
The following selection describes Cabrillo's epic voyage. It is from the *Summary Journal* of Juan Páez de Castro, a sixteenth-century Spanish historian who condensed a longer journal, now lost, probably written by a member of the expedition (from Henry R. Wagner, *Juan Rodríguez Cabrillo*).

Juan Rodríguez [Cabrillo] left the Puerto de Navidad June 27, 1542, to discover the coast of New Spain. From the Puerto de Navidad to Cabo de Corrientes it took a day and a night with a southeast wind, forty leagues. From Wednesday until the following Thursday they held their course along the coast thirty-five leagues, and Sunday, July 2, had sight of [Lower] California, having been delayed in crossing [the Gulf of California] almost four days on account of the winds. . . .

They sailed from Puerto de San Lucas [at Cape San Lucas, Lower California] Thursday night. . . . The coast is clean and without dangers. In the country inside high mountains appear, bare and broken. . . . They continued sailing along the coast, which makes a great *ensenada* [bay], the cape of which is in 26°. It is low land and sand dunes, and the coast is white and clean. . . .

Sunday, the 17th [of September], they went sailing along on their voyage, and about six leagues from Cabo de Cruz [Punta Santo Tomás] found a good closed port, having passed a small island near the mainland before reaching it. In this port they took water in a lagoon of rain water. There are some trees like silk-cotton trees except that they are of hard wood. They found some big thick logs cast up by the sea. This port is called "San Mateo" [Ensenada] and is apparently a good country, there being great savannas and grass like that of Spain. The land is high and broken. . . .

On the following Tuesday and Wednesday they sailed along the coast about eight leagues and passed by some three uninhabited islands. . . . They named them "Islas Desiertas" [now the Coronados, just south of San Diego]. On this day they saw on the mainland some great smokes. The country appears to be good, with large valleys. Inside, there are some high sierras.

On the Thursday following [September 28, 1542] they sailed about six leagues along a north-northwest coast and discovered a very good closed port in 34° 20′, which they named "San Miguel" [San Diego]. After anchoring they went ashore where there were some people, three of whom awaited them, while the rest fled. To these some presents were given, and they explained by signs that inland people like the Spaniards had passed, and they displayed much fear. That night some went ashore from the ships to fish with a net, and it seems that there were some Indians who commenced to shoot arrows at them and wounded three men.

The following day in the morning they went with the ship's boat farther up into the port, which is large, and brought back two boys who understood nothing by signs; they gave them some shirts and shortly sent them away.

The following day in the morning three large Indians came to the ships and explained by signs that some people like us, that is, bearded, dressed and armed like those on board the vessels, were going about inland. They showed by signs that these carried crossbows and swords; they made gestures with the right arm as if using lances, and went running about as if they were going on horseback, and further showed that these were killing many of the native Indians, and for this reason they were afraid. The people were well built and large and go about covered with the skins of animals.

While in this port a great tempest passed over, but nothing of it was felt as the port is so good. It was from the west-southwest and the south-southwest and violent. . . .

On Tuesday following, October 3, they left San Miguel [San Diego], and Wednesday, Thursday, and Friday sailed on their course some eighteen leagues along the coast, where they saw many valleys and plains and many smokes and sierras inland. At nightfall they were close to some islands which are about seven leagues from the mainland, and as the wind died out they could not reach them that night. Saturday, the 7th, at daybreak, they reached them, and named them "San Salvador" [now Santa Catalina] and "Vitoria" [now San Clemente].

They anchored at one and went ashore [probably at Avalon, Santa Catalina] with the ship's boat to see if there were any people there. As the boat was nearing land a great number of Indians came out of the bushes and grass, shouting, dancing, and making signs to come ashore. As from the boats they saw the women fleeing, they made signs to them not to fear; so shortly they became assured and put their bows and arrows on the ground. Launching into the water a fine canoe containing eight or ten Indians, they came out to the ships. These were given some beads and presents with which they were well pleased, and shortly went back.

The Spaniards afterwards went ashore and both the Indian men and women and everybody felt very secure. Here an old Indian made signs to them that men like the Spaniards, wearing clothes and having beards, were going around on the mainland. They remained at this island until midday.

The Sunday following, the 8th, they came to the mainland in a large bay [San Pedro Bay, the present harbor of Los Angeles], which they named "Baia de los Fumos" [Bay of Smoke] on account of the many smokes they saw there. Here they engaged in intercourse with some Indians they captured in a canoe, who made signs to them that towards the north there were Spaniards like them. The bay is in 35°; it is an excellent harbor and the country is good, with many valleys, plains, and groves of trees. . . .

Wednesday, the 18th [of October], they ran along the coast until ten o'clock and saw it all inhabited. As the wind was fresh, canoes did not come out to them. They arrived at a point like a galley which makes a cape and named it "Cabo de Galera" [Cape Galley, now Point Conception]. It is in full 36°.

As a fresh northwest wind struck them they stood off to sea and discovered two islands, one large, about eight leagues in length from east to west, and the other about four leagues. In the small one there is a good port. They are inhabited, are ten leagues from the mainland, and are called "Islas de San Lucas" [Islands of St. Luke, now San Miguel and Santa Rosa below Santa Barbara]. . . . They remained in these islands until the Wednesday following, because there was a great storm.

Wednesday, the 25th [of October], they left these islands, that is, the one farthest to windward, which has a very good port inside which no bad effects will be felt in any kind of sea weather. They named it "Posesión" [Cuyler's Harbor at San Miguel Island]. . . . On Thursday following, at vespers, the wind shifted to the south, and with this they went on their way ten leagues along a coast trending north-northwest, south-southeast. All this coast is inhabited and the land seems to be good. . . . During this month they found the weather on this coast from 34° up, like that in Spain, very cold in the mornings and afternoons and with great storms of rain, heavy clouds, great darkness, and heavy air. . . .

In all this travel they were able to avail themselves of the Indians who came on board with water and fish and displayed much friendship. In their towns they have large plazas and circular enclosures around which imbedded in the ground are many stone posts which stand about three palm-lengths above it. In the middle of these enclosures there are many very thick timbers like masts sunk in the ground. These are covered with many paintings, and we thought they must worship them because when they danced they did so around inside of the enclosure. . . .

Monday, November 13, at the hour of vespers the wind calmed down and shifted to the west. They at once set sail and turned towards land in search of their consort [the *Victoria*], praying God to succor her, as they very much feared that she would be lost. They ran to the north and to the north-northwest with a west and west-northwest wind, and the following Tuesday at daybreak had sight of land. They had to sail until the afternoon; they came to reconnoiter it in a very high country and then went along close to the coast looking for a port where they could take shelter.

The sea was so high that it was frightful to see; the coast was bold and the mountains very high. In the afternoon they lay to. The coast runs northwest-southeast.

They sighted the country at a point which projects into the sea and makes a cape: it is covered with trees and is in 40° [Point Reyes, above San Francisco].

Wednesday, the 15th, they sighted the consort [the *Victoria*], for which they gave hearty thanks to the Lord. . . . Those of the other ship had passed through even greater hardships and perils than those on the *capitana* [the flagship, the *San Salvador*], as she was small and had no covered deck. The land along which they passed is very good in appearance, but they saw neither Indians nor smokes. There are great sierras covered with snow and there is much timber. At night they took in sail and lay to.

The following Thursday, November 16, at break of day they arrived off a large *ensenada* [Drake's Bay? or Monterey Bay?], which came from behind. As it seemed to have a port and a river, they went beating about all that day and night and the following Friday until they saw that there was no river nor any haven. In order to take possession they cast anchor in forty-five fathoms, but did not dare go ashore on account of the great surf. This *ensenada* [bay] is in full 39°; all of it is full of pines down to the sea, and they named it the "Baia de los Pinos" [Bay of Pines—Drake's Bay? or Monterey Bay?].

The night following they lay to until the following day, and Saturday ran [south] along the coast and found themselves at night off Cabo de San Martín [Cape San Martin]. All the coast passed this day is very bold; there is a great swell and the land is very high. There are mountains which seem to reach the heavens, and the sea beats on them; sailing along close to land, it appears as though they would fall on the ships. They are covered with snow to the summits, so they named them the "Sierras Nevadas" [the Snow-Covered Sierras—the Santa Lucia range]. At their beginning there is a cape which projects into the sea which they named "Cabo de Nieve" [Cape Snow, now Cypress Point]. . . . Whenever the wind blew from the northwest the weather was clear.

Thursday, the 23d, they arrived on their return at the Islas de San Lucas, at the one named "Posesión" [San Miguel]. . . . While wintering at the Isla de Posesión, there passed from this present life, January 3, 1543, Juan Rodríguez Cabrillo, the captain of the ships, from a fall which he had in this island the previous time they were there, in which he broke an arm, close to the shoulder. He left as captain the chief pilot, who was one Bartolomé Ferrelo, a native of the Levant, and strongly charged him at the time of his death not to fail to discover as much as possible of all that coast. They named this island the "Isla de Juan Rodríguez" [the Island of Juan Rodríguez].

In an investigation held in Guatemala in 1560, it is stated that Cabrillo died from a broken leg, and one modern scholar conjectures that such an injury was more likely to cause gangrene and death than a broken arm.

After Cabrillo's death, his chief pilot, Bartolomé Ferrelo, took command. On February 18, 1543, Ferrelo sailed north again, and on March 1 reached latitude 42½°, opposite the Rogue River in southern Oregon. Then furious storms drove him back.

Tuesday, the 27th [of February, 1543], the wind returned to the south-southwest and lasted all that day. They ran to the west-northwest with the forecourse as it blew very strong. As it was growing dark the wind shifted to the west, and they ran all that night to the south with little sail. There was a high sea which broke over them.

On Wednesday, the 28th, at daybreak, the wind shifted to the southwest, true, but not very strong.

That day they observed the latitude in 43°. Towards night the wind freshened and changed to the south-southwest, and that night they ran to the west-northwest with great difficulty.

Thursday at daybreak the wind shifted and came from the southwest with great fury, the seas coming from many sides, which molested them very much or broke over the ships. As these had no covered decks, if the Lord had not aided them, they could not have escaped. As they could not lay to, they had to run before the wind to the northeast in the direction of land. Considering themselves lost they commended themselves to our Señora de Guadalupe and made their vows.

So they ran until three o'clock in the afternoon with great fear and travail as they saw that they were about to be wrecked. Already they saw many signs of land, which was near, such as birds and fresh logs, which came out of some rivers, although by reason of the great darkness land could not be seen.

At this hour the Mother of Our Lord succored them with the grace of Her Son, and a very strong rainstorm came up from the north, which made them run before it towards the south with lower foresails all night and all the following day until sunset. As there was a high sea running from the south, each time that it assailed them on the bow it passed over them as if over a rock. The wind shifted to the northwest and to the north-northwest with great fury, forcing them to run before it to the southeast and east-southeast until Saturday, March 3, with such a high sea that it set them wildly crying out that if the Lord and His Blessed Mother did not miraculously save them they could not escape.

Saturday at midday, the weather improved and the wind remained in the northwest, for which they gave many thanks to Our Lord. They also passed through hardships on account of the food, as they had nothing except some damaged biscuit.

Badly battered, with many men sick, the two ships returned to Navidad, Mexico, arriving April 14, 1543.

CHILDREN OF CHINIGCHINICH

As they sailed past the snow-covered mountains of California, the Spaniards did not see any black women warriors, but they did sight many red men. One-eighth of all the Indians between Mexico and Canada lived in Upper California—many just above the site of Los Angeles, around Santa Barbara. When the Indians in the Los Angeles area all lit their campfires at the same time, they produced . . . smog!

The California Indians were happy, peaceful, and primitive. They dwelled in small communities of several hundred persons each, gathering acorns or catching salmon and other fish for food. They built crude houses, which, in the north, were half caves, and they made baskets and dugout canoes. Above all, they enjoyed their numerous dances. They had a Black Bear Dance, a New Clover Dance, a War Dance, a White Deer Dance, a Welcome ("Glad to see you!") Dance—so many dances, with singing, that life seemed one long birthday party. (Each baby was greeted with a Newborn Child Dance.)

Their culture was of the Stone Age. Their tools were sharp mussel shells or elk-horn wedges. They had no knowledge of the wheel or of writing. Their dress was scanty—a loincloth, or nothing, for the men, a tule grass skirt for the women. They were rather short, broad-faced, and flat-nosed. But they had made an intelligent adaptation to their environment, with its plentiful food supply and comparatively mild climate. In the centuries since they arrived from Asia, by way of the Bering Strait and Alaska, they had survived and increased and now numbered about 150,000. For them, before the white man came, perhaps California *was* an earthly paradise.

The following selection, about their occupations and childbirth customs, is from *Chinigchinich*, by Father Geronimo Boscana, a Franciscan friar who came to California from Spain in 1814; the translation is by Alfred Robinson (from Alfred Robinson, *Life in California*, 1846).

Their occupation consisted in the construction of the bow and arrow, in hunting for deer, rabbits, squirrels, rats, &c., which not only provided them with food, but *clothing*, if so it can be called. Their usual style of dress was a small skin thrown over the shoulders, leaving the remaining portion of their person unprotected; but the females formed a kind of cloak out of the skins of rabbits, which were put together after this manner. They twisted them into a kind of rope, that was sewed together, so as to conform to the size of the person, for whom it was intended, and the front was adorned with a kind of fringe, composed of grass, which reached down to the knees; around the collar it was adorned with beads, and other ornaments, prized by the Indians.

They passed their time in plays, and roaming about from house to house, dancing and sleeping; and this was their only occupation, and the mode of life most common amongst them from day to day. The old men, and the poorer class, devoted a portion of the day to constructing house utensils, their bows and arrows, and the several instruments used in making their baskets; also nets of various dimensions, which were used for sundry purposes, such as for catching fish and wild fowl, and for carrying heavy burdens on their backs, fastened by a strap passed across the forehead. In like manner, the females used them for carrying their infants.

The women were obliged to gather seeds in the fields, prepare them for cooking, and to perform all the meanest offices, as well as the most laborious. It was painful in the extreme, to behold them, with their infants hanging upon their shoulders, groping about in search of herbs or seed, and exposed as they frequently were to the inclemency of the weather. Often it was the case that they returned home severely fatigued, and hungry, to cook the fruits of their toil, but, perhaps, there would be no wood, the fire extinguished, and their lazy husband either at play or sleeping, so that again they would be obliged to go out into the cold for fuel.

When the brutal husband came home, or awoke from his sluggishness, he expected his meal, and if not prepared at the moment, invectives and ill treatment were the universal consequence. Poor creatures! more unfortunate than slaves! They were in such subjection, that for the most trifling offence, punishment was the result, and oftentimes death. . . . The most wonderful of God's blessings enjoyed among them, was the great facility with which they underwent their accouchement [childbirth], when it would seem as if they endured no suffering. . . .

The first time the wife became enceinte [pregnant], it was the custom to give a grand feast to all in the town, and they passed the whole of one night in dancing and singing. This rejoicing was on account of the looked-for increase, and in their songs they asked of Chinigchinich [their god], his clemency towards the unborn, for the female was good—having, in a short time, arrived to a state that gave hopes of her becoming a mother. They looked upon a sterile woman as being unfortunate—one who would ever meet with calamities.

On the day of the birth of the child, they made no particular demonstration of satisfaction, except to exhibit the infant to the people. If it were a male, the grandfather named it, saying A.B., thus shall he be named. If it were a female, then the grandmother named it, and generally gave it her own name, or that of the mother, unless some event occurred about the time of the birth, and then it was given a name which would serve to commemorate that event. . . .

The most ludicrous custom among these Indians, was that of observing the most rigid diet from the day of their wives' confinement [for childbirth]. They could not leave the house, unless to procure fuel and water—were prohibited the use of all kinds of fish and meat—smoking and diversions; and this observance lasted generally from fifteen to twenty days.

NOVA ALBION

After Cabrillo's voyage, Upper California seemed to be lost again in the northern fogs. But in the second half of the century ships of another nation appeared in the Pacific, and one of them touched on California. These were England's pirates and privateers, aiming to "annoy" the King of Spain by attacking his New World possessions.

The first and most famous of all the Elizabethan raiders was Sir Francis Drake. In 1579, in his heavily armed *Golden Hind*, Drake fell upon the defenseless Spanish settlements in Chile, Peru, and Central America. Off Ecuador he captured a Spanish treasure ship carrying silver worth several million dollars. Then Drake fled north, as the Spaniards conjectured he would, to "the region of the Californias." On June 17, 1579, he entered a bay (now called Drake's Bay) just above San Francisco and thus became the first Englishman to set foot on California.

Drake overhauled and cleaned the *Golden Hind* here and waited for the typhoon season in the Far East to pass, before continuing his voyage around the world. He also passed the time by claiming all northern California for Elizabeth I. He interpreted a ceremony in which the native Indian chief placed a "crown" of feathers on Drake's head as a gift of the sovereignty of the land. Apparently he thought of it as a possible way station for future English voyagers to the Far East by way of the mysterious "Strait of Anian" across Canada.

He named the territory Nova Albion—New England. (Albion is an ancient name for England.) The following selection states Drake's claim to the land. It is from *The World Encompassed* (1628), an anonymous account of Drake's circumnavigation, based on notes left by the chaplain of the expedition, Francis Fletcher.

> Our General [Drake], with his gentlemen and many of his company, made a journey up into the land, to see the manner of [the Indians'] dwelling, and to be the better acquainted with the nature and commodities of the country. Their houses . . . being many of them in one place, made several villages here and there.
>
> The inland we found to be far different from the shore, a goodly country, and fruitful soil, stored with many blessings fit for the use of man. Infinite was the company of very large and fat Deer which there we saw by thousands, as we supposed, in a herd; beside a multitude of a strange kind of Conies [rabbits—actually, ground squirrels], by far exceeding them in number.
>
> Their heads and bodies, in which they resemble other Conies, are but small; his tail, like the tail of

a Rat, exceeding long; and his feet like the paws of a . . . mole; under his chin, on either side, he hath a bag, into which he gathereth his meat, when he hath filled his belly abroad, that he may with it, either feed his young, or feed himself when he lists not to travel from his burrow. The people eat their bodies, and make great account of their skins, for their king's holiday coat was made of them.

This country our General named *Albion*, and that for two causes; the one in respect of the white banks and cliffs, which lie toward the sea; the other, that it might have some affinity, even in name also, with our own country, which was sometime so called.

Before we went from thence, our General caused to be set up a monument of our being there, as also of her Majesty's and successors' right and title to that kingdom; namely, a plate of brass, fast nailed to a great and firm post; whereon is engraven her grace's name, and the day and year of our arrival there, and of the free giving up of the province and kingdom, both by the king and people, into her Majesty's hands: together with her Highness' picture and arms, in a piece of sixpence current English money, showing itself by a hole made of purpose through the plate; underneath was likewise engraven the name of our General, etc.

The Spaniards never had any dealing, or so much as set a foot in this country, the utmost of their discoveries reaching only to many degrees Southward of this place.

THE MANILA GALLEON

In 1565, Spain began to occupy the Philippine Islands. The great navigator Andrés de Urdaneta made this possible by discovering a return route to Mexico that avoided the headwinds of the lower latitudes. Urdaneta's route was from Manila northeast toward Japan, then east to Cape Mendocino, above San Francisco. Here the galleons turned south, keeping the coast in sight much of the way down to the straggling village of Acapulco, Mexico, where they unloaded their goods.

Thus the Spaniards sailed right past the coast of California but did not stop to explore its fertile valleys or look for gold in its rugged mountains.

The Manila galleon which made the annual voyage to Acapulco was a floating treasure chest of spices, silks, wax, porcelain, chinaware, perfumes, jewelry, and amber. Merchants, officers, and even common sailors made from 200 to 400 percent profit on these Eastern luxuries. But the economic boom which might have been sparked by trade between Spanish America and the Philippines was stifled by the mercantilist ideas of the day. Such a boom would have caused a rush to the Philippines *and* to Upper California as a crossroads on the return route.

But colonies were supposed to benefit the mother country, not to become independently prosperous. Merchants of Seville, who had a monopoly of trade with Spanish settlements, would have liked the China goods to reach Mexico and Peru by a 10,000-mile detour through their city. These merchants had laws passed that limited the trade between Manila and Acapulco to one 500-ton galleon per year and forbade transshipment of goods from Acapulco to Peru. So California remained isolated and undeveloped.

The outward voyage from Mexico to Manila was an easy journey of three months. But the return trip took twice as long and was full of hardship and danger. The terrors of this voyage from Manila to the California coast are described in the following selection, by an Italian traveler, Gemelli Careri (from Careri's *Voyage Round* the World, in *A Collection of Voyages and Travels,* ed. Awnsham and John Churchill).

The voyage from the Philippine Islands to America may be called the longest, and most dreadful of any in the world; as well because of the vast ocean to be crossed, being almost the one half of the terraqueous globe, with the wind always ahead; as for the terrible tempests that happen there, one upon the back of another, and for the desperate diseases that seize people, in seven or eight months lying at sea, sometimes near the line, sometimes cold, sometimes temperate, and sometimes hot, which is enough to destroy a man of steel, much more flesh and blood, which at sea had but indifferent food. . . .

The poor people stowed in the cabins of the galleon bound towards the Land of Promise of New Spain, endure no less hardships than the children of Israel did, when they went from Egypt towards Palestine. There is hunger, thirst, sickness, cold, continual watching [wakefulness], and other sufferings; besides the terrible shocks from side to side, caused by the furious beating of the waves.

I may further say they endure all the plagues God sent upon Pharaoh to soften his hard heart; for if he was infected with leprosy, the galleon is never clear of an universal raging itch, as an addition to all other miseries. If the air then was filled with gnats; the ship swarms with little vermin, the Spaniards call *Gorgojos* [weevils], bred in the biscuit; so swift that they in a short time not only run over cabins, beds, and the very dishes the men eat on, but insensibly fasten upon the body.

Instead of the locusts, there are several other sorts of vermin of sundry colours, that suck the blood. Abundance of flies fall into the dishes of broth, in which there also swim worms of several sorts. In short, if Moses miraculously converted his rod into a serpent; aboard the galleon a piece of flesh, without any miracle, is converted into wood, and in the shape of a serpent.

I had a good share in these misfortunes; for the boatswain, with whom I had agreed for my diet, as he had fowls at his table the first days, so when we were out at sea he made me fast after the Armenian manner, having banished from his table all wine, oil and vinegar; dressing his fish with fair water and salt.

Upon flesh days he gave me *Tasajos Fritos*, that is, steaks of beef or buffalo, dried in the sun or wind, which are so hard that it is impossible to eat them, without they are first well beaten like stockfish; nor is there any digesting them without the help of a purge. At dinner another piece of that same sticky flesh was boiled, without any other sauce but its own hardness, and fair water. At last he deprived me of the satisfaction of gnawing a good biscuit, because he would spend no more of his own [provisions], but laid the king's allowance on the table; in every mouthful whereof there went down abundance of maggots and *Gorgojos* chewed and bruised. . . .

The tediousness [length] of the voyage is the cause of all these hardships. 'Tis certain, they that take this [voyage] upon them, lay out thousands of pieces of eight [pesos], in making the necessary provision of flesh, fowl, fish, biscuit, rice, sweetmeats, chocolate, and other things; and the quantity is so great, that during the whole voyage, they never fail of sweetmeats at table, and chocolate twice a day, of which last the sailors and grummets [cabin boys] make as great a consumption, as the richest. Yet at last the tediousness [length] of the voyage makes an end of all; and the more, because in a short time all the provisions grew naught, except the sweetmeats and chocolate, which are the only comfort of passengers. Abundance of poor sailors fell sick, being exposed to the continual rains, cold, and other hardships of the season. Yet they were not allowed to taste of the good biscuit, rice, fowls, Spanish bread and sweetmeats, put into the custody of the master by the king's order, to be distributed among the sick; for the honest master spent all at his own table.

Notwithstanding the dreadful sufferings in this prodigious voyage, yet the desire of gain prevails with many to venture through it, four, six, and some ten times.

THE FINDING OF MONTEREY

As more English privateers found their way into the Pacific, the worries of the Spanish viceroys of Peru and Mexico increased. In 1587 a reckless young English aristocrat, Thomas Cavendish, even succeeded in capturing one of the rich Manila galleons near Lower California. Thereupon, Viceroy Luis de Velasco, of Mexico, decided to act.

In 1595, Velasco ordered Sebastian Cermeño to look for a good port in Upper California on his journey back from the Philippines—a port that could be a fortified base. But Cermeño's ship, the *San Agustín*, was wrecked in Drake's Bay, just above San Francisco, and Cermeño and his crew were fortunate to get back to Mexico in a makeshift launch.

In 1602 the new viceroy, the Conde de Monterey, dispatched the aggressive merchant Sebastian Vizcaíno on the same mission. Vizcaíno left Acapulco, Mexico, on May 5, 1602, with three ships, the *San Diego*, the *Santo Tomás*, and the *Tres Reyes*. In a voyage lasting ten and a half months, he reached the same latitude as Cabrillo —Cape Blanco, in southern Oregon. He also discovered, below San Francisco, a bay which he praised highly and named Monterey after the viceroy.

Although Monterey was destined to become the capital of Spanish California, the most lasting result of the voyage was the names the self-assertive Vizcaíno bestowed on places Cabrillo had visited and named before. Thus Cabrillo's San Miguel became San Diego (Vizcaíno had a mass said there on November 12, St. James' feast day); San Salvador became Santa Catalina (sighted by Vizcaíno on St. Catherine's feast day); Galley Point became Point Conception, and so on. Vizcaíno gave us our map of California.

Three white-mantled Carmelite friars went on Vizcaíno's expedition, and one of them, Father Antonio de la Ascensión, wrote an account of the voyage which was widely read. The following selection, describing the finding of Monterey, is from Father Antonio de la Ascensión's *Brief Report of the Discovery in the South Sea* (from H. E. Bolton, *Spanish Exploration in the Southwest 1542–1706*).

> After we left the Port of San Diego we discovered many islands placed in a line, one behind another [the Santa Barbara Islands]. Most of them were inhabited by many friendly Indians, who have trade and commerce with those of the mainland. It may be that they are vassals of a petty king who came with his son from the mainland in a canoe with eight oarsmen, to see us and to invite us to go to his land, saying that he would entertain us and provide us with anything which we needed and he possessed. He said that he came to see us on account of what the inhabitants of these islands had reported to him.
>
> There are many people in this land, so many that the petty king, seeing that there were no women on

the ships, offered by signs to give to everyone ten women apiece if they would all go to his land, which shows how thickly populated it all is. And besides, all along, day and night, they made many bonfires, the sign in use among them to call people to their land. Since there was no convenient port where the ships could be secure in the country whence this petty king came, the acceptance of his invitation was deferred until the return voyage.

Thereupon we went forward with our voyage, and at the end of some days arrived at a fine port, which was named Monterey [December 16, 1602]. It is in latitude 37°, in the same climate and latitude as Seville. This is where the ships coming from the Philippines to New Spain come to reconnoitre. It is a good harbor, well sheltered, and supplied with water, wood, and good timber, both for masts and ship building, such as pines, live oaks, and great white oaks, large and frondose [leafy], and many black poplars on the banks of a river that near by enters the sea and was named the Carmelo. In climate, in birds and game, in variety of animals and trees, in everything it is essentially like our Old Spain.

When the ships from China [the Philippines] arrive at this place they have already sailed four months and they come in need of repairs, which in this harbor they can make very well, and with perfect convenience; therefore it would be a very good thing for the Spaniards to settle this port for the assistance of navigators, and to undertake the conversion to our Holy Faith of those Indians, who are numerous, docile, and friendly. And from here they might trade and traffic with the people of China and Japan, opportunity for that being favorable because of propinquity.

The land of this country is very fertile and has

good pastures and forests, and fine hunting and fowling. Among the animals there are large, fierce bears, and other animals called elks, from which they make elk-leather jackets, and others of the size of young bulls, shaped and formed like deer, with thick, large horns. There were many Castilian roses here. There are pretty ponds of fresh water. The mountains near this port were covered with snow, and that was on Christmas day. On the beach was a dead whale, and at night some bears came to feed on it.

There are many fish here, and a great variety of mollusks among the rocks; among them were certain barnacles, or large shells, fastened to the lowest part of the rocks. The Indians hunt for them to extract from them their contents to eat. These shells are very bright, of fine mother-of-pearl [probably abalone].

All along this coast, there is a great abundance of sea-wolves or dogs [probably sea lions], of the size of a yearling calf. They sleep on the water, and sometimes go ashore to take the sun; and there they place their sentinel in order to be secure from enemies. The Indians clothe themselves in the skins of these animals, which are healthful, fine, beautiful, and convenient. . . .

We set sail from here after dispatching the admiral's ship to New Spain with the news of what had been discovered and with the sick who were unfit for service. Among them returned Father Tomás de Aquino, one of the three religious who were going in this fleet, because he had been ill many days, and in order that the sick might have someone to confess them should God desire to relieve them of this life. Our departure in quest of Cape Mendocino was made on the first Sunday after Epiphany [January 5], of the year 1603. On the coast we noted the port of San Francisco [Drake's Bay, not our San Francisco], where in times past there was lost a ship from China which was coming with orders to explore this coast [the *San Agustín* of Cermeño]. I believe that much of the wax and porcelain which the vessel carried is there to-day.

And we arrived at Cape Mendocino in latitude 42°, which is the highest latitude at which the China ships sight land. Here, because of the severity of winter in this climate, and of the cold, and the stiffness of the rigging, and because almost all the crew were ill, the sails were lowered. The captain's ship got into the trough of the sea, and, as it could not be steered, the currents that run to the Strait of Anian whose entrance begins here, carried it little by little toward land. In eight days we had ascended more than one degree of latitude, which was up to 43°. . . . No one landed here, as all the crew were very ill, only six persons being able to walk.

Here the coast and land turns to the northeast, and here is the head and end of the realm and mainland of California and the entrance to the Strait of Anian. If on this occasion there had been on the captain's ship even fourteen sound men, without any doubt we should have ventured to explore and pass through this Strait of Anian, since all were of good courage to do this. But the general lack of health and of men who could manage the sails and steer the ship obliged us to turn about toward New Spain, to report what had been discovered and seen, and lest the whole crew should die if we remained longer in that latitude.

Father Ascensión was confident not only that a fleet could reach the "Strait of Anian" but also that California itself was an island. The "Strait of Anian," he believed, had its entrance near the northern shore of this island.

Along the eastern edge of the Sierra Nevada he placed an elongated Gulf of California, like a moat separating California from the rest of North America.

Father Ascensión depicted California as an island in a map he made in 1620—and for more than a hundred years Europe believed him! It was as though Ordóñez de Montalvo's mythical "island named California" had come back to haunt men's imaginations. In 1699 the Jesuit missionary Father Eusebio Kino concluded that Lower California is a peninsula, but few listened to him. Europe was not really convinced until 1746, when Father Fernando Consag sailed all the way around the Gulf of California and thus proved that the gulf did *not* extend into Upper California. The next year, 1747, Ferdinand VII of Spain handed down his verdict. By a royal decree he declared: "California is not an Island."

THE VICEROYS LOOK NORTH

Early in the seventeenth century, blond Dutch captains, who sailed their ships in squadrons, followed in the wake of the English pirates in the Pacific. The viceroy of Peru raised a fleet to fight against these *Pechelingues*, as the Dutch were called (from their home port of Vlissingen). The viceroy of Mexico built a fort to protect Acapulco, twice visited by the Dutch raiders. And more plans were submitted to the Spanish government for the settlement of the Californias.

Spaniards had now conquered Mexico almost to its present northern limits, of upper Chihuahua and upper Sonora. Pearl fishers were busy in the stormy Gulf of California and were always promising to explore the peninsula in return for their licenses. But these pearl seekers were not really interested in pioneering on that arid, mountainous strip of land. And in northern Chihuahua and northern Sonora, the Spaniards faced the flaming arrows of the Apache.

The Apache blocked the trail from Sonora to the mouth of the Colorado River and then, by the "back door" of desert and mountain pass, into Upper California. The barrenness of Lower California discouraged the establishment of a base there—from which the Spaniards might have marched north to San Diego. A third route to Upper California, by sea, meant a voyage taking as long as that to the Philippines, with extra vessels to transport supplies.

The viceroys looked north, but after Juan de Oñate's conquest of New Mexico, completed in 1605, the hard-pressed Spanish government could not find money to finance a further advance. In 1697 the Jesuits, under Father Juan María Salvatierra, finally began the occupation of Lower California but did not permit other Spaniards to come because their presence would hinder the conversion of the Indians.

Early in the eighteenth century the Spanish government ordered the Californias settled—but nothing happened. The Jesuits still barred Spaniards from their territory. The Manila galleon still sailed past the hills of Monterey without stopping. In 1742, when Spain and England were again at war, George Anson seized one of these galleons near the Philippines. Then, in 1757, Father Andrés Burriel publicized the dangers to Spain's possessions in a sensational, widely read work, *Noticia de la California.*

Burriel warned that Spain must occupy the Californias immediately or lose the Philippines, Mexico, and New Mexico; a foreign power entrenched in California astride the shipping lanes from the Philippines and on the flank of Mexico could overthrow much of Spain's Pacific empire. His work was translated into English, French, Dutch, and German. Just a few years later an Italian pamphlet described Russian explorations in northwest America. Reports from the Spanish embassy in Moscow confirmed the Russian advance toward California. The Russians were coming!

At last, Spanish officials were galvanized into action. The government sent José de Gálvez, a man of great vision and energy, as *visitador-general* (Inspector-general) of New Spain, with supreme power. The settlement of California was about to begin.

2
Father Serra and the Missions

From that hill Padre Serra left for the New World, There one day to spread the faith, even in its most distant part.
—*Hymn sung in Majorca*

Fray Junípero Serra

The Anza Expedition, painting by Walter Francis

"THE GRAY OX"

In the early eighteenth century California was still at the end of the known world. But its isolation was being threatened; more and more ships which did not fly the red and yellow standard of Castile were coming to the north Pacific.

The Dane Vitus Bering, sailing for Russia, reached his strait between Siberia and Alaska in 1728 and 1741. In 1742 the Englishman George Anson threatened the Philippines. French, Dutch, and Portuguese vessels also arrived.

Fortunately for Spain, just at this time (1749) there came to the New World a small Franciscan friar, Junípero Serra, who was destined to win Upper California for the threatened Spanish Empire.

Father Serra called himself "The Gray Ox." He had given up a good position as professor of theology in Majorca (a Spanish island in the Mediterranean) to come to the New World as a missionary. Father Serra was short and swarthy—very patient, very humble, and very dedicated. In his gray Franciscan robes, with the heavy white cord at his waist, Father Serra was prepared to walk from one end of California to the other to convert the Indians to Christianity.

The following selection gives a portrait of Father Serra as he appeared on his voyage from Cádiz to Mexico. It is from Francisco Palou's *Life of Fray Junípero Serra* (1787, tr. Reverend M. J. Geiger), a popular biography by a fellow Franciscan which helped establish Father Serra's fame.

The first group of missionaries embarked from Cádiz on August 28, 1749. It comprised the president . . . and twenty other friars, among whom was my venerated father [Serra]. On the long voyage of ninety-nine days which it took to reach Veracruz, many inconveniences and scares befell us. . . . Because of the scarcity of water . . . during the fifteen days preceding our arrival at Puerto Rico . . . the amount they gave us each twenty-four hours was hardly more than a pint, so that it was impossible even to make chocolate.

But Fray Junípero [Serra] suffered these inconveniences with such patience that he was never heard to utter the least complaint. . . . His companions . . . were wont to ask him if he were not thirsty. To this he answered: "It is nothing to worry about."

And if anyone complained that he could not stand the thirst, he would answer with great affability and with still greater instruction: "I have found a means to avoid thirst, and it is this: to eat little and talk less in order not to waste the saliva." . . .

We arrived at the Island of Puerto Rico to take on water in the middle of October. . . . We sailed out of that port for Veracruz on November 2, and when we were already within sight of it (at the end of the same month) there arose a hurricane so violent that we were obliged to head toward the Sound of Campeche. On the way thither we ran into such a violent storm lasting through December 3 and 4, that during the night of the 4th we gave ourselves up for lost.

We had no other recourse than to prepare ourselves for death. But our Fray Junípero, in the midst of that great storm, retained as undisturbed a peace and as tranquil a mind as if he were experiencing the most serene day.

When he was asked if he were afraid, he answered: "A little." But when he remembered the purpose for which he had come to the Indies, even this fear left him immediately.

After the Franciscans prayed to St. Barbara, "the tempest ceased" and they landed at Veracruz. Then Father Serra, as a pious sacrifice to God, walked from Veracruz to Mexico City with one companion friar (263 miles), while the others rode. Father Serra was bitten by some impious—and very fierce—mosquitoes on the way. One leg became infected and gave him trouble for the rest of his life.

THE FIRST SETTLERS

Soon after he arrived in Mexico, Father Serra was sent to Sierra Gorda ("Fat Mountain") to preach to the Indians there. This misty range is in the part of Mexico below Texas. Father Serra spent nine years there; he walked up and down the hills a distance longer than that from New York to San Francisco.

In 1768, when Father Serra had returned to Mexico City and was teaching in the Franciscan College of San Fernando there, alarming news reached the Spanish Minister of State. The Minister of State immediately relayed it to Inspector-General José de Gálvez, in Mexico: Russians, it was said, had landed in northwest America and fought a pitched battle with Indians there.

The rumor was false, but the energetic Gálvez promptly interpreted this message from the home country as an order to defend Upper California. He prepared not one but four separate expeditions to head north and settle the land immediately; two would go by land, two by sea.

All would depart from Lower California, the marchers from Loreto, the small ships *San Carlos* and *San Antonio* from La Paz.

Three hundred men, including soldiers, friars, craftsmen, sailors, and Indian converts ("neophytes"), would go. Gaspar de Portolá, a captain of the crack Spanish Dragoons, was the commander in chief. Father Serra was asked to go with Portolá and was made father president of the missions of Upper California.

A member of the force on the *San Carlos*, the capable army engineer Miguel Costansó, kept a journal of the push north. The following selection, describing the arrival of the first settlers at San Diego, is from Miguel Costansó's *Narrative of the Portolá Expedition* (from *Publications of the Academy of Pacific Coast History*, Vol. I, No. 4, March, 1910).

> The *San Carlos* . . . entered the Port of San Diego on the 29th of April [1769], one hundred and ten days after its departure from La Paz. But its crew and the troops on board . . . arrived in a deplorable condition. Scurvy had attacked all without exception, so that . . . two men had already died of this disease, while the majority of the crew and half of the soldiers were confined to their beds. Only four seamen were remaining on their feet. . . .
>
> The packet *San Antonio,* although it sailed one month after the *San Carlos,* had the good fortune to complete the voyage in fifty-nine days, and had been in the Port of San Diego since the 11th of April. But half of its crew was likewise afflicted with the scurvy, of which, also, two men had died. Amid so much sickness, all experienced great happiness in being reunited; and . . . the officers resolved by common consent to devote themselves to the immediate relief of the sick.

The first task was to look for a watering-place where a supply of good water could be obtained to fill the barrels for the use of the men. For this purpose, the officers, Don Pedro Fages, Don Miguel Costansó, and the second captain of the *San Carlos,* Don Gorge Estorace, landed on the 1st of May, with twenty-five of the soldiers and seamen. . . .

Skirting the western shore of the port, they observed at a short distance, a band of Indians armed with bows and arrows, to whom they made signs by means of white cloths. . . . But the Indians, regulating their pace according to that of our men, would not, for more than half an hour, let themselves be overtaken. Nor was it possible for our men to make greater speed because they were weak. . . .

At last we succeeded in attracting [the Indians] by sending toward them a soldier, who, upon laying his arms on the ground and making gestures and signs of peace, was allowed to approach. He made them some presents, and meanwhile the others reached the Indians, and completely reassured them by giving them more presents of ribbons, glass beads, and other trifles. When asked by signs where the watering-place was, the Indians pointed to a grove . . . to the northeast, giving to understand that a river or creek flowed through it, and that they would lead our men to it if they would follow.

They walked for about three leagues till they came to the banks of a river lined on both sides with over-spreading cottonwoods of heavy foliage. Its bed was about twenty yards wide, and it emptied into a lagoon which at high tide could accommodate the launch. [The river was later called the San Diego River.] . . .

Having examined the watering-place, the Spaniards returned on board the vessels. . . . Close to the beach, on the east side of the port, a small enclosure was [then] built with a parapet of earth and brushwood, and mounted with two cannon. Some sails and awnings were landed from the vessels and, with these, two tents suitable for a hospital were made. On one side were placed the tents of the two officers, the missionaries, and the surgeon. When everything was ready to receive the sick, they were brought on shore in the launches, and were housed in the tents as comfortably as possible. . . .

Nothing [so far] had been heard of the land expedition. . . . On the 14th of May, however, the Indians informed some of the soldiers who were on the beach, that other similarly armed men were approaching from the south . . . and explained very clearly by signs that they were mounted on horses. This news caused great rejoicing to all, and was soon found to be true, when the men and the pack-train of the first division of the land-expedition [under Fernando de Rivera y Moncada] were sighted.

They exchanged salutes by joyful volleys from their muskets. . . . The whole land-expedition arrived without having lost a single man or even carrying one person sick after a journey of two months. . . . All [then] moved to the new camp which was transferred one league further north on the right bank of the river, on a hill of moderate height.

A MULETEER DOCTOR

"The cross before the sword," Gaspar de Portolá, first governor of Upper California, was to say.

Father Junípero Serra, "The Gray Ox," bore the cross. On March 28, 1769, the fifty-five-year-old Serra painfully mounted his mule and rode north from Loreto, in Lower California. Portolá was awaiting him at Santa María, the northernmost frontier mission, with the second land expedition.

Father Serra was accompanied by a soldier guard and two servants—and his provisions were a loaf of bread and a piece of cheese! However, he could obtain more food at each of the missions the Jesuits had founded, flung like a rosary up the long, narrow peninsula. At these stops he also collected silver chalices, a silver shell to hold the water used in baptism, white satin altar cloths, and Sanctus bells for his future missions.

By the time he came to Santa María his leg was much worse. Nevertheless, Father Serra set out with Portolá and his men. Within ten days, as he wrote, "The inflammation reached halfway up the leg." The brave Franciscan could neither ride nor walk. It appeared that he would be left behind and would never see the greener lands to the north.

The following selection, describing this crisis, is from Francisco Palou's *Life of Fray Junipero Serra* (1787, tr. Reverend M. J. Geiger).

[After the first two days of the journey, Father Serra] could neither stand nor sit, but had to lie down in bed, suffering such pain that it was impossible for him to sleep.

When the governor [Portolá] saw him in this condition, he said to him: "Father President, Your Reverence now sees how incapable you are of accompanying the expedition. . . . If Your Reverence wishes, we shall carry you to the first mission, where you can recuperate, and we will continue on our journey."

But our Venerable Father . . . answered him in this

way: "Let Your Honor not speak of this, for I trust that God will give me the strength to arrive at San Diego. . . . But even though I die on the road, I will not turn back. . . ."

[Then] the governor . . . ordered a litter constructed, fashioned in the manner of a stretcher or bier for carrying the dead, and made of rods, so that he [Father Serra] might be laid thereon and be carried by the neophyte Indians. . . . When the Venerable Father heard of this, he became very sad . . . [considering] the great labor involved in his being carried by those poor Indians. . . .

He called the muleteer Juan Antonio Coronel and said to him: "Son, do you know how to prepare a remedy for the wound in my foot and leg?"

But the muleteer answered him: "Father, what remedy could I know of? Do you think I'm a surgeon? I'm a muleteer; I've healed only the sores of the animals."

"Well then, son, just imagine me to be an animal, and that this wound is the sore of an animal from which have developed this swelling of the leg and the great pains I experience. . . . Make me the same remedy which you would apply to an animal."

The muleteer smiled . . . [but] replied: "Father, I shall do so in order to please you."

He obtained a little tallow and crushed it between two stones and mixed it with herbs . . . and when he had fried this, he applied it to the foot and leg . . . in the form of a plaster.

God worked in such a way . . . that he [Father Serra] slept that night through till morning and that he awoke so relieved from his pain and wound that he arose to say Matins and Prime as he customarily did. . . . In order to go on with the expedition not the least delay had to be made on his account.

MISSION SAN DIEGO DE ALCALA

Father Serra and the Portolá expedition—last of the four—reached San Diego on July 1, 1769. The shores of the sheltered bay did not look like a new settlement but more like an open-air hospital.

One-third of the 300 men who had started from Lower California had died, chiefly from scurvy on the ships. A number of the Indian converts had deserted. Many of the remaining men were stretched out, ill, in makeshift huts on a small hill overlooking the San Diego River and the sparkling bay.

In spite of the sickness in camp, Governor Portolá was determined to march on to Monterey. He chose the seventy-three healthiest men left, including Fathers Crespi and Gómez, and departed July 14, 1769. Fathers Serra, Parron, and Vizcaíno, with a handful of soldiers, remained in San Diego among the sick.

On July 16, two days after Portolá left, a cross was raised against the blue California sky on the small hill, later called Presidio Hill. Father Serra preached a sermon; the first mission, San Diego de Alcala, and the first settlement, San Diego, were formally established and the history of Upper California began.

The following selection, narrating some of Father Serra's problems with the Indians, is from Francisco Palou's *Life of Fray Junípero Serra* (1787, tr. Reverend M. J. Geiger).

The missionaries tried by means of gifts and kind treatment to attract the pagans who presented themselves. But since these did not understand our language, they paid attention to nothing else but to accepting what was given them, provided it was not food. Food they absolutely would not taste, so that if a piece of something sweet was placed in a boy's mouth, he would immediately spit it out as if it were poison. Of course, they attributed the illness of our men to the food, which they had never seen. . . .

If their aversion to our food was great, their desire for our clothing was no less notable. They even went so far as to steal as many articles of clothing as they could lay hands on. . . . Not even the sails of the ship were safe from theft.

One night they had rowed up to it in their tule-boats, and there they were found cutting off a piece of a sail; on another occasion they did the same in regard to a cable which they wanted to take with them. It was therefore resolved to put aboard a guard of two soldiers . . . but at the mission the guard was decreased. . . .

They observed all these activities sharply. They were ignorant of the force of firearms and trusted in the strength of their numbers, as well as in their arrows and wooden instruments, fashioned like sabres, which cut like steel. They also had instruments such as clubs or wooden mallets. . . . So they began to rob without fear. . . . They were willing to take a chance and by putting all of us to death they would take home the spoils. . . .

On the 15th [of August] . . . after the Venerable Father President and Father Vizcaíno had finished saying Mass . . . a large number of pagans, armed for war, fell upon the place and began to plunder whatever they found, stealing from the sick even the sheets with which they were covered. The corporal of the guard sounded the alarm immediately.

When the Indians saw the soldiers putting on their leather jackets and defensive armor . . . and making ready their muskets, they started to flee and shot their arrows; meanwhile, the four soldiers, the carpenter and the blacksmith began to fire valiantly.

The blacksmith especially, who doubtless was full

of extraordinary spirit because he had just received Holy Communion . . . went in between the houses or huts, shouting: "Long live the Faith of Jesus Christ, and may these dogs, enemies of that faith, die!" At the same time he fired on the pagans.

Father Vizcaíno was wounded in the hand, and the friars' Indian servant, Joseph María, was killed, but then the pagans were driven off. In a few days they returned, bringing their wounded, whom the surgeon of the expedition charitably treated. The Indians now showed "fear and respect" for the Spaniards and "frequented the mission but came without carrying any arms."

An Indian lad of fifteen years . . . came almost every day. . . . Our Fray Junípero endeavored . . . to teach him something of our language in order to see whether by this means he might be able to confer Baptism on some of the children. . . .
Within a few days a pagan came accompanied by many others, carrying in his arms a young child, and according to the signs he made he gave him to understand that he wanted it baptized. Our Venerable Father was filled with joy and immediately brought forth some clothing to dress the child. He invited the corporal of the guard to act as godfather, and the other soldiers to attend and solemnize the first baptism, at which the Indians also were present.
When the Venerable Father was finished with the [preliminary] ceremonies and just as he was about to pour the water, the pagans snatched the child and carried it away to their village, leaving the Venerable Father with the shell [containing the baptismal water] in his hand. At that moment he had to use all his prudence not to show resentment . . . and to restrain the soldiers from avenging the profanation. . . .

The grief of Our Venerable Father at being frustrated in baptizing that child was so great that it lasted for many days. . . . When he would relate this incident, even many years later, he had to dry the tears running from his eyes, and he would end by saying: "Let us give thanks to God, that now so many have been made Christians without the least repugnance on their part."

This was indeed so, for he lived to see in that Mission San Diego 1,046 baptized, both children and adults. . . . And among the baptized were many of those who attempted to take his life in the beginning.

Father Serra had been very eager to achieve a spiritual "first"—the first baptism in Upper California. He was disappointed that this honor fell to Fathers Crespi and Gómez, with the Portolá expedition; they baptized two dying Indian infant girls on July 22, 1769, on their way to Monterey.

THE SEARCH FOR MONTEREY

When Portolá and his men marched north, they were looking for a bay "very secure against all winds . . . all that can be desired for commodiousness and as a station for ships making the voyage to the Philippines." So Sebastian Vizcaíno had described the port he had found in 1602. Portolá imagined a large harbor, like a lake, opening out behind bottleneck headlands.

Unfortunately, as the Spaniards would learn, the superport described by Vizcaíno existed only in his salesman's imagination. As the Portolá expedition wound northward over the coastal hills, Miguel Costansó, the engineer, described the hardships borne by the Spanish soldiers. He also gave interesting details of the life of the Indians around Santa Barbara, the most densely populated part of Upper California.

The following selection is from Miguel Costansó's *Narrative of the Portolá Expedition* (from *Publications of the Academy of Pacific Coast History*, Vol. I, No. 4, March, 1910).

The soldiers . . . use two sorts of arms—offensive and defensive. The defensive arms are the leather jacket and shield. The first, whose shape is like that of a coat without sleeves, is made of six or seven plies of white tanned deerskin. . . . The shield is made of two plies of raw bull's hide. It is carried on the left arm and with it they turn aside spears and arrows, the rider not only defending himself, but also his horse.

In addition to the above they use a sort of leather apron . . . which, fastened to the pommel of the saddle, hangs down on both sides, covering their thighs and legs, that they may not hurt themselves when riding through the woods.

Their offensive arms are the lance—which they handle adroitly on horseback—the broadsword, and a short musket which they carry securely fastened in its case. They are men of great fortitude and patience in fatigue; obedient, resolute, and active, and we do not hesitate to say that they are the best horsemen in the world. . . .

It must be borne in mind that the marches of this [expedition] . . . through unknown lands and on unused roads, could not be long. Not to mention other reasons that made it necessary to halt and camp early —the necessity of reconnoitering the country from day to day in order to regulate the marches according to the distance between the watering-places, and consequently to take the proper precautions. . . .

Stops were made, as the necessity demanded, at intervals of four days, more or less, according to the extraordinary hardships occasioned by the greater roughness of the road, the labor of the sappers, and the straying of the animals . . . [and] to accommodate the sick when there were any—and in course of time there were many. . . .

But the pack-animals themselves constitute the greatest danger on these journeys and are the most dreaded enemy. . . . At night, and in a country they do not know these animals are very easily frightened. The sight of a coyote or fox is sufficient to stampede them—as they say in this country. A bird flying past, or dust raised by the wind is likely to frighten them and to make them run many leagues, throwing themselves over precipices and cliffs. . . . This expedition, however, suffered no serious detriment on this account, owing to the care and watchfulness which were always observed. . . .

In order and manner described, the Spaniards made their marches over vast territories which became more fertile and more pleasant the further they penetrated to the north. In general, the whole country is inhabited by a large number of Indians, who came forth to receive the Spaniards, and some accompanied them from one place to another. They are very docile and tractable, especially from San Diego onward.

The Indians observed to have the greatest energy and industry are those who inhabit the islands and the coast of the channel of Santa Barbara. They live in towns, the houses of which are spherical in form, like the half of an orange, are covered with reeds, and are as much as twenty yards in diameter. Each house contains three or four families. The fireplace is in the middle, and in the upper part of the house they leave an air-passage or chimney for the escape of the smoke....

The expertness and skill of these Indians is unsurpassed in the construction of their canoes of pine boards. They are from eight to ten yards in length from stem to stern-post, and one yard and a half in breadth. No iron whatever enters into their construction, and they know little of its use. But they fasten the boards firmly together, making holes at equal distances apart, one inch from the edge, matching each other in the upper and lower boards, and through these holes they pass stout thongs of deer sinews. They pitch and calk the seams, and paint the whole with bright colors.

They handle them with equal skill, and three or four men go out to sea to fish in them, as they will hold eight or ten [men]. They use long double-bladed oars, and row with indescribable agility and swiftness....

Their language is sonorous and easy to pronounce. Some [of our people] believed that they could discover in it a certain relation to the Mexican.... But those who have command of the Mexican will be better able to judge from the following words:

Words in that language

Nucchú	head
Kejuhé	breast
Huachajá	hand
Chipucú	elbow
Apa	village
Temi	chief
Amo	no
Pacá	one
Excó	two
Maseja	three

SAN FRANCISCO BAY

Above Santa Barbara, the land changed. There were no more Indian towns consisting of houses shaped "like the half of an orange." There were scarcely any Indians. The terrain was all wilderness—deep canyons, towering hills, a tangle of brush through which a road must be hacked, bleak cliffs that blocked the route along the shore. Icy northwest gales roared in from the sea. Fog clung to the trees and blanketed the mountains. Everywhere appeared the tracks of the dangerous grizzly bear.

At last, the Spaniards emerged at the "Point of Pines," a tongue of land covered with heavy evergreens that projects into the Pacific and forms the southern rim of Monterey Bay. Portolá, his officers, and Fathers Gómez and Crespi conferred; they scratched their heads, but could not believe that this horseshoe-shaped identation was Vizcaíno's Monterey. Hungry and sick though they were, they voted to continue the search up the coast.

A little over a week later, from a hilltop, a scouting party under Sergeant José Ortega sighted the faint blue headland of Point Reyes, thirty miles to the north. There lay "the port of San Francisco," as the Spaniards called small Drake's Bay, just above the present city. They had come too far—they had missed Monterey.

Ortega and his men stared, bitterly disappointed. They noted that between them and Point Reyes was "a great arm of the sea," extending inland "as far as the eye could reach"—twenty miles and more. It was an obstacle that Portolá's men, in their weakened condition, could never hope to get around. And, anyhow, they were not looking for Drake's Bay.

So Portolá at last gave up, and turned back toward San Diego. Only slowly, in the months that followed, did the Spaniards come to realize that in that "great arm of the sea" Sergeant Ortega had stumbled upon the finest harbor in the western Americas, later to become one of the world's great seaports, San Francisco Bay.

The following selection, narrating the discovery of San Francisco Bay, is from the manuscript narrative of Father Juan Crespi (from George Davidson, *The Discovery of San Francisco Bay*).

[We saw] a very great gulf or bay, and at its entrance six or seven headlands . . . and also Point Reyes extending a great distance into the sea, and which forms, as it were, an island . . . all about the port. . . . Furthermore, this port has ravines and by the middle one an estuary runs into the land. . . .

We arrived at this port the night of All Saints Day [November 1, 1769] and we said mass on that day, and on All Souls Day. Notwithstanding we explored for three days, and passed onward to see if we could pass around this estuary.

This estuary is not really such, but a great arm of the sea, which extends inland at least eight leagues. In its narrow part it is three leagues wide, and in its widest stretch it will not fall short of four; in one word, it is an exceedingly large and most famous port, which could not only contain all the navies of His Catholic Majesty, but those of all Europe as well. . . .

We made our camp before the end of this estuary about one league distant from it in a plain of at least six leagues in extent, covered with oaks and some evergreens. We camped near a good stream of water which runs into the estuary. The land is all very good. . . . Señor Ortega went out with soldiers to explore for four days, by order of the Governor [Portolá], and in all those four days could not finish the circuit of this estuary to the other side. . . .

This very great estuary or arm of the sea has its

communication between some high mountains, and which they say has three islands; which we could not see from where we were, being on low ground. And they say that this estuary is surrounded on all sides by high mountains . . . so that it is like a lake, protected against all winds. And considering that this most famous estuary has in its narrowest parts three leagues in width . . . it seems therefore its depth should be great, and that ships drawing much water could enter. . . .

Consequently if in time the ships do not discover the Bay of Monterey . . . in default of it we have this most famous [bay] . . . wherein to plant the standard of the Most Holy Cross, and to convert to Our Holy Catholic Faith the very numerous docile and gentle heathen who occupy the borders of this estuary.

Before departing for Upper California, Father Serra is said to have talked about the names of the new missions with Inspector General Gálvez. Gálvez suggested San Diego, San Carlos (at Monterey, in honor of King Charles III of Spain), and San Buenaventura (between San Diego and Monterey). Father Serra was troubled.

"Is there to be no mission in honor of Our Holy Father, St. Francis?" he asked.

"Let St. Francis find the port bearing his name and he will have his mission there," Gálvez retorted.

Through Sergeant Ortega, St. Francis had now complied with the inspector-general's request.

BELLS IN THE WILDERNESS

Not long after the discovery of San Francisco Bay, Father Serra founded the mission of San Carlos at Monterey (1770) and then the mission of St. Anthony of

Padua (1771), inland and south of Monterey. When Father Serra chose the spot for the mission of St. Anthony, he showed himself to be a true follower of St. Francis.

St. Francis had loved the good earth—all life. In his "Song of the Creatures," St. Francis had thanked God for "all His creatures, especially our brother the sun . . . our sister the moon . . . our brother the wind . . . and [even] our sister, the death of the body." Father Serra now rang his mission bells from a wilderness tree with this same Franciscan joy, as related below.

The following selection is from Francisco Palou's *Life of Fray Junípero Serra* (1787, tr. Reverend M. J. Geiger).

They inspected the terrain and found an extensive and attractive plain in that same valley adjoining a river, which they named the San Antonio. To them it seemed quite an apt site for the new mission because of the good current of water flowing even in the month of July, which is the high point of the dry season. They realized that they could readily utilize the river for irrigation purposes. They all concurred in the choice . . . whereupon the Venerable Father [Serra] ordered the mules to be unloaded and the bells hung from the branch of a tree.

As soon as they could be rung, the servant of God began to sound them in a merry peal and to shout as if enraptured: "Come, you pagans; come, come to the Holy Church; come, come to receive the Faith of Jesus Christ."

One of the two fathers who had been assigned by the president, Father Fray Miguel Pieras, seeing this spectacle, said to him: "Why do you tire yourself here if this is not to be the spot where the church is to be built? Nor is there a single pagan anywhere hereabouts. It is a waste of time to ring the bells."

"Father," answered Fray Junípero, "allow my overflowing heart to express itself. Would that this bell were heard throughout the world . . . or at least, that it were heard by every pagan who inhabits this sierra."

They immediately constructed a large cross and, after it had been blessed, venerated it. They then hoisted it and set it up on that very spot. At the same time, they built a shelter and set up within it the altar table. There the Venerable Father celebrated the first Mass in honor of St. Anthony, the patron of that mission, July 14, 1771. . . .

There was one pagan present at this divine Sacrifice, who, attracted either by the sound of the bell or the novelty of seeing such strange people, had come along as the Mass was being celebrated. The venerable priest adverted to this when he turned towards his congregation for the sermon after the Gospel. His heart full of joy, he . . . [said]:

"I trust in God and in the patronage of St. Anthony, that this, his mission, shall become a great town of many Christians; for we behold here what was not seen at any mission so far founded: that at the first Mass the first fruits of paganism were present. Nor will he [the pagan] fail to communicate to the other pagans what he has seen here."

It turned out thus, as we shall afterwards see.

THE DESERT ROAD—BACK DOOR
TO CALIFORNIA

At first, San Francisco Bay was thought to be an extension of Drake's Bay. But gradually, emphasis shifted to the great bay itself. In 1775, Juan Manuel Ayala sailed through the Golden Gate, and in the same year Juan

Bautista de Anza was ordered to found two missions and a presidio on its shores.

The two expeditions of Juan Bautista de Anza represented a new approach to Upper California. Anza did not come by sea or by the Lower California peninsula. He slipped in by the "back door"—across the Colorado River and Colorado Desert and over the mountains to San Gabriel Mission (near Los Angeles). He opened the door in 1774; in 1775 he brought 240 colonists safely past the treacherous dunes and through the rugged mountains without the loss of a single man or woman.

Anza's trail was the best road to Upper California. It avoided the headwinds and the great distance of the sea voyage; it originated not in barren Lower California, which could scarcely feed its own few settlers, but in prosperous Sonora, the "bread basket" of Mexico. It might have been widened to a freeway, over which people and supplies flowed in abundance; then it would have linked Upper California as closely to Mexico as gleaming transcontinental rails later bound the Atlantic and Pacific coasts.

But this dream of Anza's, which was also the dream of the outstanding new viceroy, Antonio Bucareli, was not to be. The Yuma Indians slammed the door shut. In 1781 they massacred all the soldiers and friars in two small settlements on the Colorado River, as well as all the soldiers and male colonists of a large band on the way to Upper California. When the Spaniards failed to conquer the rebellious Yuma, they abandoned the settlements, gave up the route, and fell back on the uncertain sea transport. Upper California remained isolated and relatively unpopulated—until the arrival of aggressive Anglo-Saxons after 1821.

The failure was not Anza's fault. He had pleaded for the establishment of a presidio at the Colorado River. His kindness to the Yuma actually kept them from joining the

San Diego Indians in the 1775 uprising which might have ended Spanish occupation of Upper California. Anza was a great leader and frontiersman—a gallant Spanish officer, considerate of his men, energetic and resourceful. He was the forerunner of Lewis and Clark and the covered wagons.

The following selection tells about Anza's battle with the sand dunes and his arrival at San Gabriel on his first expedition (1774). It is from Anza's *Complete Diary* (from Herbert Eugene Bolton, *Anza's California Expeditions*, Vol. II).

Tuesday, February 15.—At seven o'clock in the morning the march was begun toward the west-northwest along the trail by which the Indians said we should arrive at the watering place near the sierra [Signal Mountain, Arizona]. . . . After going a little more than a league [three miles] we found a pool of very salty water.

From here we went on another league through a sand dune and found another well of water very limited in quantity, but more potable [drinkable]. . . . Having examined this we went forward by the trail mentioned, but it led us into some very dense sand dunes and we became lost entirely, because the wind moves the dunes about and carries the sand in various directions.

For this reason it was now necessary to leave half of the load at the last well mentioned [called elsewhere the "Deep Well of Little Water"] . . . on account of the worn-out condition in which the mules arrived.

On ordering that this should be done and that a sufficient guard should remain with it, I suggested to the two fathers who accompanied me that . . . it would be best to send back half of the load and half of the soldiers, to the village of the Yumas . . . to await us on the return; and that with the other half, less embarrassed [encumbered], we should be able to effect our arrival in Northern California. [Father Garcés opposed this plan, so Anza did not divide his forces, but he did leave the half-load at the Deep Well of Little Water.]

All this having taken place, we again took up the march, and at half past eleven, after having crossed many sand dunes we came to another, larger and higher, which it was necessary to cross in order to reach the small range where they told us the water hole was. It appeared that the range was about five leagues away, and that in the weak condition of the riding animals they would not be able to get over the sand dunes, and much less the loaded mules.

Therefore, because another peak was visible toward the south and nearer, in which direction it was seen that the sand dune might be circumvented, and because Father Garcés assured me that very close to it there was a large village where he had been two years before, having an abundance of water and pasturage and which he called San Jacome, I decided to go to it. So I sent orders to . . . the pack train and the riding animals which were coming behind [to turn south toward San Jacome].

Father Garcés went with Father Díaz and two soldiers to seek San Jacome, but they could not find it. Anza then decided to go back to the Deep Well of Little Water, and from there on back to his starting point, Santa Olaya, Arizona.

After resting at Santa Olaya, Anza made a second start and succeeded in outflanking the sand dunes by taking a long detour along the base of some mountains to the south. Then the Spaniards traveled northwest across Borrego

Valley and up into the San Jacinto Mountains, toward Los Angeles.

From a pass here, Anza saw ahead "most beautiful green and flower-strewn prairies, and snow-covered mountains with pines, oaks, and other trees which grow in cold countries. Likewise here the waters divide, some flowing this way toward the Gulf [of California] and others toward the Philippine Ocean [the Pacific]." On March 22, 1774, he reached his destination.

Tuesday, March 22.—At seven o'clock today we continued our march and went three leagues northwest . . . then . . . five more to the west-northwest and also to the west, in order to free ourselves from many places miry with water that comes from the sierra on our right which we have mentioned.

Having covered this distance we crossed the river that runs close to the mission of San Gabriel, where I arrived at sunset and announced myself to the corporal of the guard of this new establishment. . . .

We found here four friars, its missionaries, from the College of San Fernando de Mexico, who welcomed us with unrestrained jubilation and demonstrations of joy, with solemn peal of bells and chanting of the *Te Deum*. . . . This was all the more pleasing to them because it was so unexpected, for they had not had any news, except very remote, of this expedition, which they had considered impracticable even for a hundred men.

Even though the friars and the soldiers saw us, they could hardly believe that people could have come from Sonora, and they kept repeatedly asking me if it were true, tears springing to their eyes, caused by the joy and pleasure at seeing this expedition accomplished, and at knowing how close at hand Sonora was and how easy the transit from it.

THE MARTYRDOM OF FATHER JAYME

On the night of November 4, 1775, the infant colony of Upper California seemed to be flourishing. Only a few Spaniards were scattered through it, like needles in a haystack of Indians. But five tiny missions—at San Diego, Los Angeles, San Luis Obispo, and two at Monterey—needed only to be connected to make the future Camino Real, or King's Highway.

Father-President Serra, having founded four of the missions, was settled at Monterey, busy with plans for more. The gallant Anza was shepherding the first group of colonists from Sonora through the mountains behind Los Angeles. Viceroy Antonio Bucareli was preparing a settlement on the shores of the "port of ports," San Francisco Bay.

But also on that brilliant, moonlit night more than a thousand angry Indians, who had collected in the hills in back of San Diego, crept through the shadows. They were coming down the valley of the San Diego River, toward mission and presidio—brown-skinned nomads, gripping bows and arrows and knotty clubs, clad in nothing but their hatred for the Spaniard. Hatred for the rough soldiers who had pursued their wives—even hatred for Father Luis Jayme and his strict mission discipline.

At one thirty in the morning they neared the mission, which had been moved several miles up the valley, where the land opened out so that crops could be raised. There they separated into two bands. One band bypassed the mission, with its bright fire burning in front of the guardhouse—it was chilly. This group continued down the valley toward the presidio.

The others hid in the arroyo just beyond the mission. They were supposed to remain there until they saw flames from the presidio, then attack. But they gripped their clubs with such fury it was not certain they would wait.

What followed is narrated in the following selection, from Francisco Palou's *Life of Fray Junípero Serra* (1787, tr. Reverend M. J. Geiger).

More than a thousand Indians gathered together. Many of them were not known one to another, nor had they even seen one another, but they were simply invited by the others. They agreed to separate into two bodies, one to fall upon the mission, the other upon the presidio. . . . Thus agreed, and well armed with arrows and clubs, they set forth. . . .

They arrived in the valley of the San Diego River on the night of November 4. There they separated. Half of them . . . marched towards [the presidio]. The others, without being detected, approached the houses where the neophytes [Indian converts] lived at the mission. A group of armed pagans was stationed at each house of the neophytes to prevent anyone from escaping or giving the alarm, threatening them with death if they should.

The greater number of them went to the church and sacristy to rob clothing, church goods and whatever else they wanted. Others with firebrands which they found in the barracks of the soldiers—of whom there were only three and a corporal, and evidently all were asleep—began to set fire to the barracks and to all the rooms. As a result of this and the terrifying cries of the pagans, all awoke.

The soldiers sprang to arms, while the Indians were already shooting their arrows. The priests were sleeping in separate rooms. Father Fray Vincente came forth and on beholding the fire went over to where the soldiers, together with two small boys, the son and nephew of the lieutenant in command of the presidio, were gathered. In another room lived the blacksmith and carpenter of the mission, as well as the carpenter of the presidio, who had come to the mission because of illness. . . .

Father Fray Luis [Jayme], who slept in another small room, on hearing the noise of the shouts and the crackling of the fire, came out and, seeing a great number of Indians, approached them, greeting them in the accustomed manner: "Love God, my sons." The Indians realized he was a priest, and as wolves do to a young lamb, they laid hold of him, while he bore himself as one mute, not opening his lips.

They conducted him through the thickets of the arroyo, where they divested him of his holy habit. In his naked state, they began to strike the Venerable Father with their clubs and shot countless arrows into his body. . . . There remained not a sound portion of him except his consecrated hands. This was the condition in which he was found at the place where he was killed.

The handful of Spaniards at the mission now barricaded themselves in the kitchen, which was protected by adobe walls on three sides. They piled up trunks of clothing along the fourth, open side. The Indians deluged them with "arrows, stones, chunks of adobe, and firebrands," but they held out until dawn, when the Indians fled. The presidio had not been attacked after all.

Reinforcements were rushed south from Monterey and also from San Gabriel—Anza rode to the rescue, with seventeen of his soldiers. They reached San Diego none too soon.

Upper California was thus saved for Spain—but just barely. Meanwhile, the Russians stood on the threshold of Alaska—and were looking south.

3
The Russian Bear

> We shall be able little by little to expand farther south to the port of San Francisco ... and ... at the slightest concurrence of favorable political circumstances in Europe, include [the coast of California] among the Russian possessions.
> —NIKOLAI REZANOV,
>   Letter to the Directors of the
>   Russian-American Company, 1806

Fort Ross

FUR TRADERS FROM THE NORTH

Tall Russians in beaver hats were said to have come to North America already. That rumor woke the Spaniards from their siesta and brought them to Upper California in 1769. Was the rumor true?

Not at that moment—but it was a prophecy. In 1769 the Russians stood at the shore of the Pacific; they had pushed their frontier 5,000 miles across Siberia in only sixty years (1579–1639). And from Siberia they could walk almost to Alaska, around the rim of the Pacific Ocean, which is like a great upside-down bowl. The Dane Vitus Bering, sailing for Russia, had found this out in 1728 and 1741, when he discovered the narrow strait that separates Siberia and Alaska.

Besides, there is a shortcut just below the Bering Strait, straight across from the Kamchatka Peninsula of Siberia to southern Alaska—a path of stepping-stone islands. These are the Aleutians, which are really the peaks of drowned mountains. In 1769 Russian fur traders were in the Aleutians and sending the Aleuts out to hunt sea otter in their skin-covered boats.

In 1784 the Russians settled Kodiak, the last "stepping-stone." By the end of the century they were below Alaska, at the island of Sitka in what is now British Columbia. They were looking south toward the Columbia River and the grainfields of California, which might supply food for frozen Russian America.

These Russian fur traders (*promyshlenniki*) were big, burly trappers and hunters—quarrelsome, hard-drinking, and independent, like our mountain men. They endured exile from home, 50-below-zero weather, and the hostility of the Alaskan Indians (Tlingis) because they hoped to become rich. Not only Russia but China paid high prices for their furs—especially for the beautiful deep brown fur of the sea otter, frosted at the tips of the hairs. One sea otter pelt sold in the China market brought as much money as a clerk could earn in a year.

Now the czar's government became interested in these Russian pioneers in the New World. It decided to organize them in a company which would have government support but still be a semiprivate corporation. In doing this, the czar was taking a leaf out of Great Britain's book of empire building. His Russian-American Company would be like the British East India Company—private merchants who had penetrated and governed India, preparing the way for Great Britain to claim the country.

Nikolai Rezanov, a former guardsman who was now a career official, was the man most responsible for the formation of the Russian-American Company. In 1794 the czar had sent this alert, well-educated son of an impoverished aristocrat to be in charge of the first colonists dispatched to Russian America. ("Russian America" came to include the Aleutians, Alaska, and northwest America, all anchored on Sitka—"New Archangel.") Rezanov was so enthusiastic that in 1799 he persuaded the czar to establish the company, with a twenty-year monopoly on hunting, trading, and discovery.

Thus far the Russians only claimed the land as far as 55° north latitude (now northern British Columbia). But before and after 1800 the Russian traders, acting on government orders, buried imperial markers—plates with the inscription "Land Belonging to Russia"—all the way south to San Francisco Bay.

Also, in 1803 Nikolai Rezanov set out on a round-the-world tour on which he would not only seek a trade treaty with Japan but would visit California and see for himself how strong the Spanish fortifications were. He looked forward eagerly to counting Spanish cannon, but he did not anticipate looking into the dark eyes of the most beautiful girl in the Californias, Concepción Argüello.

REZANOV AND CONCHA

One foggy morning in March, 1806, the schooner *Juno* slipped into San Francisco Bay. It had come down from New Archangel, below Alaska, under the command of Nikolai Rezanov. Its seamen were very sick with scurvy.

Rezanov peered into the mist, praying that the Spaniards would give them fresh fruits and vegetables, perhaps in exchange for the manufactured goods the *Juno* carried. He recalled bitterly how last year the Japanese had made him wait for six months in a house that was like a cage, then told him no thanks, they would not trade with Russia!

As soon as the fog thinned and the rugged hills, the white presidio, and mission of San Francisco were revealed, Rezanov sent his physician-companion Dr. Georg von Langsdorff ashore with several officers. Spanish officers and a priest clad in gray robes met them there. The Spaniards and Russians could not understand each other until the priest tried some Latin. Von Langsdorff replied in the same language, and the Franciscan's face lit up like the sunrise.

Then the temporary commander, young Don Luis Argüello, not only gave them permission to land but invited Rezanov and his officers to breakfast in the Argüello home. (It was probably lucky for Rezanov that Don Luis' father, the commandant, and strict Governor José Arillaga both were away in Monterey that day.)

An hour or so later Rezanov was being introduced to Concepción Argüello, Don Luis' sister. The tall, pale

Russian, standing a head taller than the Spaniards, with a fur cape hanging from one shoulder and his tunic covered with the czar's decorations, was a romantic figure.

As for fifteen-year-old Concepción—"Concha"—Dr. von Langsdorff for once forgot to be stuffy and scientific when he described her: "She was distinguished by her vivacity and cheerfulness, her love-inspiring and brilliant eyes, her excellent and beautiful teeth, her smiling expression and beautiful features, her shapeliness of figure and for a thousand other charms including an artless, natural demeanor."

Concha was beautiful, and she was restless. "California is a beautiful place with a warm climate, much grain and cattle—and nothing else!" Concha would say, with a toss of her head.

What did Concha and Nikolai think of each other when they met? A distinguished California novelist, Gertrude Atherton, re-created the scene. The following selection, with imagined dialogue but based on authentic history, is from Gertrude Atherton's *Rezanov* (1906).

>[Rezanov's] eyes during Argüello's declamation had wandered with a singular fidelity to the beautiful face of the eldest daughter of the house. She had responded with a humorous twinkle in her magnificent black eyes and not a hint of diffidence. . . . He was the first man of any world more considerable than the petty court of the viceroy of Mexico that had visited California in her time, and excellent as she found his tall military figure and pale cold face, the novelty of the circumstance fluttered her more.
>
>Doña "Concha" Argüello was the beauty of California, and although her years were but sixteen her blood was Spanish, and she carried her tall deep figure and fine head with the grace and dignity of an accomplished woman. She had inherited the white skin and delicate Roman-Spanish profile of the Mora-

gas, but there was an intelligent fire in her eyes, a sharp accentuation of nostril, and a full mobility of mouth . . . that betrayed a strong cross-current forcing the placid maternal flow into rugged and unexplored channels. . . .

As Rezanov . . . walked directly over to her, she smilingly seated herself on a sofa and swept aside her voluminous white skirts. She was not sure that she liked him, but in no doubt whatever of her delight at his advent.

Her manners were very simple and artless, as are the manners of most women whom Nature has gifted with complexity and depth.

"It is now two years and more that we have been excited over the prospect of this visit," she said. "But, if you will tell me what you have been doing all this time, I, at least, will forgive you; for you will never be able to imagine, señor, how I long to hear of the great world. I stare at the map, then at the few pictures we have. I know many books of travel by heart; but I am afraid my imagination is a poor one, for I cannot conjure up great cities filled with people —thousands of people! Dios de mi alma! A world where there is something besides mountains and water, grain fields, orchards, forests, earthquakes, and climate? Will you, señor?"

"For quite as many hours as you will listen to me. I propose a compact. You shall improve my Spanish. I will impart all I know of Europe—and of Asia— if your curiosity reaches that far."

"Even of Japan?" There was a wicked sparkle in her eye.

"I see you already have some knowledge of the cause of my delay." His voice was even, but a wound smarted. "It is quite true, señorita, that the first embassy to Japan, from which we hoped so much, was a humiliating failure, and that I was played with for six months by a people whom we had regarded as a nation of monkeys...."

Underneath the polished armour of a man who was a courtier when he chose and the dominating spirit always, he was hot and quick of temper. His light cold eyes glowed with resentment at the dancing lights in hers, as he cynically gave her a bald abstract of the unfortunate mission. He reflected that commonly he would have fitted a different mask to the ugly skull of fact, but this young barbarian, as he chose to regard her, excited the elemental truth in him, defying him to appear at his worst. He was astonished to see her eyes suddenly soften and her mouth tremble.

"It must have been a hateful experience—hateful!" Her voice, beginning on its usual low soft note, rose to a hoarse pitch of indignation. "I should have killed somebody! To be a man, and strong, and caressed all one's life by fortune—and to be as helpless as an Indian! Madre de Dios!"

"I shall take my revenge," said Rezanov shortly; but the wound closed, and once more he became aware of the poignant sweetness of Castilian roses. Concha wore one in her soft dusky hair, and another where the little round jacket of white linen, gaily embroidered with pink, met on her bosom. But if sentiment tempted him he was quickly poised by her next remarks. She uttered them in a low tone, although the animated conversation of the rest of the party would have permitted the two on the sofa to exchange the vows of love unheard.

"But what a practice for your diplomatic talents, Excellency! Poor California! At least let me be the first to hear what you have come for?" Her voice dropped to a soft cooing note, although her eyes twinkled. "For the love of God, señor! I am so bored in this life on the edge of the world! To see the seams and ravelings of a diplomatic intrigue! I have read and heard of many, but never had I hoped to link my finger in anything subtler than a quarrel between priest and Governor, or the jealousy of Los Angeles for Monterey. I even will help you—if you mean no harm to my father or my country. And I am not a friend to scorn, señor, for my blessed father is as wax in my hands, the dear old Governor adores me, and even Padre Abella, who thinks himself a great diplomat, and is watching us out of the corner of his eye, while I make him believe you pay me so many compliments my poor little head turns round—Bueno señor!" As she raised her voice she plucked the rose from her dress and tossed it to Rezanov. Then she lifted her chin and pouted her childish lips at the ironical smile of the priest.

A DIPLOMAT IN LOVE

Dr. Georg von Langsdorff, Rezanov's physician, observed that "the bright sparkling eyes of Doña Concepción had made a deep impression" on the former guardsman. But Rezanov remained a diplomat even when he had to confess his love.

He wrote an account of his visit to California for the Secretary of Commerce, in St. Petersburg. When Rezanov came to his betrothal, he did not describe Concha's bright eyes. Instead, he said that through her he might obtain trading rights for his company. Concha would be a kind of food stamp entitling the Russians to buy wheat in California.

The following passage, giving Rezanov's view of the courtship (at least, for official publication), is from Rezanov's *Report of His Voyage* (from *The Rezanov Voyage to Nueva California in 1806*, ed. T. C. Russell).

Here I must lay open to your excellency some purely personal affairs. Seeing that our situation was not getting better, expecting every day that some serious unpleasantness would arise, and having but little confidence in my own men, I decided that I should assume a serious bearing where I had before been but formally polite and gracious.

Associating daily with and paying my addresses to the beautiful Spanish señorita, I could not fail to perceive her active, venturesome disposition and character, her unlimited and overweening desire for rank and honors, which, with her age of fifteen years, made her, alone among her family, dissatisfied with the land of her birth. She always referred to it jokingly; thus, as "a beautiful country, a warm climate, an abundance of grain and cattle,—and nothing else."

I described Russia to her as a colder country, but still abounding in everything, and she was willing to live there, and at length I imperceptibly created in her an impatient desire to hear something more explicit from me, and when I proffered my hand, she accepted.

My proposal was a shock to her parents, whose religious upbringing was fanatical. The difference in religion, besides the prospective separation from their daughter, was, in contemplation, a dreadful blow to them.

They sought the counsel of the misioneros, who did not know what to do. The parents forced their daughter to church and had her confessed. They urged her to refuse me, but her brave front finally quieted them all. The holy padres decided to leave the final decision to the throne of Rome.

Not being able to bring about the marriage, I had a written conditional agreement made, and forced a betrothal. Consent was given on condition that the agreement be kept secret pending the decision of the pope. Thereafter my deportment in the house of Commandante Argüello was that of a near relative, and I managed this puerto [port] of his Catholic majesty as my interests called for. . . . .

Should fate decree the completion of my romance, —not begun in hot passion, which is not becoming at my age, but arising under the pressure of conditions,—remoteness, duties, responsibilities,—perhaps also under the influence of remnants of feelings that in the past were a source of happiness in my life,— then, and in such case, I shall be in a position to serve my country once again, as by a personal examination of the harbor of Vera Cruz, Mexico, and by a trip through the interior parts of America. This could not be accomplished by, nor would permission be granted to, any one else.

PLANS FOR CONQUEST

Rezanov's love for Concha, and their betrothal, thus did not cloud his vision of a Russian empire in the north Pacific. Like the *promyshlenniki* who had won Siberia, this taut aristocrat would marry a woman of the land he planned to conquer. One secret of the Russians' success was their willingness to practice "togetherness."

So in letters written *after* his betrothal, Rezanov explained how Russia could take over Concha's California. The following passages are from his letter to the Secretary of Commerce and his report to the directors of the

Russian-American Company (from S. B. Okun, *The Russian-American Company*).

> If the [czarist] government had given earlier thought to this part of the world . . . if it had continued to follow the perspicacious views of Peter the Great who . . . had planned the Bering expedition with something definite in mind, then one could positively maintain that New California would never have become a Spanish possession, since the Spaniards turned their attention to California only in 1760 and it is only through the spirit of enterprise of the missionaries that they have forever secured for themselves this tract of the finest land.
> Today there is only one unoccupied stretch [north of San Francisco], so useful to us and quite necessary, and if we should allow it to slip out of our grasp, what will posterity say?

> We shall be able little by little to expand farther south to the port of San Francisco which marks the boundary of California. . . . If only the means are provided for the early beginnings of this plan, I can boldly say that we shall attract people to Columbia from various places, and shall have so consolidated our position at the end of ten years as ever to have in mind the coast of California and, at the slightest concurrence of favorable political circumstances in Europe, include it among the Russian possessions. . . .
> The Spanish are quite weak in that area, and if in 1798, when war was declared on the Spanish court, our company had had the power corresponding to its activities, it would have been an easy matter to utilize the part of California from the 34th parallel of north latitude as far as the mission of Santa Barbara and keep that piece of land forever, since,

because of a condition of nature itself, it would have been impossible for the Spanish to receive any assistance from Mexico by land.

Rezanov dreamed of Russian traders descending along both sides of the Pacific, turning the north Pacific into a Russian lake. Russia would rule from the Amur River in China to Santa Barbara. The modern scholar S. B. Okun gives a good summary of these expansionist plans, in the following selection (from S. B. Okun, *The Russian-American Company*).

> The Tsarist Government set before the Russian-American Company certain tasks of great political importance. It was to be the aim of the Company to realize the grandiose plan of expansion as a result of which the northern part of the Pacific would become "an inland sea" of the Russian empire.
>
> This plan presupposed the further entrenchment of Russia along the west coast of North America, including California, the Hawaiian Islands, the southern part of Sakhalin and the mouth of the Amur [in China]. These colonies, together with Kamchatka, Alaska, and the Aleutians, which already belonged to Russia, were to make that country the all-powerful master of the whole northern Pacific.
>
> California, apart from its strategic importance, was also to serve as an agricultural base for the Russian colonies in America. The Hawaiian Islands, which constitute the principal naval base for all vessels plying between American and Asiatic ports, would, in case they came into the hands of Tsarist Russia, bring under its control all the seaborn [*sic*] trade with China. Furthermore, it was proposed to establish cotton plantations on the Hawaiian Islands and to export all kinds of spices from there.
>
> It was, in short, a plan for direct colonial conquest.

SIBERIAN WINTER

Steep mountain slopes, impenetrable forest, marsh, and muskeg bog. Then the high, snow-whipped plateau of eastern Siberia. A packtrain plods across the desolate landscape; Cossacks and beasts huddle low against the icy winds. Before, they had been drenched by the fall rains, and their leader, Nikolai Rezanov, had had to lie in bed for weeks, his eyes glazed with fever, in a peasant's hut.

The trouble was that after writing his enthusiastic letters about conquering California, Rezanov had delayed his homeward journey. First, he had to outfit a tender at Sitka; it was going to raid Japan—this one, lonesome ship—to get revenge for the way the Japanese had snubbed Russia (and Rezanov) in the matter of the trade treaty. So he was caught by the rains when he started overland from the Pacific coast of Siberia to Irkutsk, the chief inland city. The 2,200-mile trip had taken him five months.

But he wouldn't stop there until spring. On to St. Petersburg—on to obtain the czar's permission for his marriage —and the Pope's—and the Spanish king's!

Early March, 1807—the dead of the Siberian winter. ... Nikolai Rezanov, white and thin as a ghost under his great coat, sways on his horse. He must complete the negotiations and return to Concha within two years, as promised. Concha waits for him. ...

Feverishly, Rezanov urges his stumbling mount on toward a blurry stand of larches on the bleak horizon—a little shelter there—just ahead, through the fine snow.

But the horse lurches, and Nikolai loses his balance. His shoulder hits the frozen ground; he feels a sharp pain as the horse's hoof catches him squarely in the temple; then all goes black. ...

Nikolai Rezanov, architect of empire, was buried by his Cossacks in remote Krasnoyarsk. And Concha, dreaming of the czar's court, waited in the presidio of San Francisco

—waited perhaps six years before learning the truth. Then she quietly folded her dreams, refused all other suitors, and, years later, joined the Dominican sisters.

FORT ROSS—LITTLE RUSSIA IN CALIFORNIA

Other Russians, however, shared Rezanov's expansionist ideas. The northwest coast of America was a vacuum, drawing trappers and traders of three nations. After Rezanov's death—perhaps because this dynamic leader was gone—traders from Canada and the United States got to the Columbia River in Oregon ahead of the Russians. The *promyshlenniki* seemed blocked.

But in 1811 Dr. Georg von Langsdorff suggested that the best place for a Russian settlement was California itself. The following selection is from his *Voyages and Travels* (1811), translated by T. C. Russell (from *Langsdorff's Narratives of the Rezanov Voyage*, ed. T. C. Russell).

If Russia would engage in an advantageous trade with these parts [Upper California], and procure from them supplies for her northern establishments, a colony of her own planted here is the only way to bring it about. In a country blessed with such a mild climate as California is, where there is such an abundance of wood and water, with so many other means for the support of life, and an excellent harbor, persons of an enterprising spirit might in a few years establish a very powerful colony.

With the service of skilled mechanics now to be found in Sitka, in Norfolk Sound, several kinds of wind and water mills could soon be constructed, looms made, and distilleries erected. Large and small vessels, and storehouses for foodstuffs, would then be built; vast herds of cattle would be raised, and sea-otters taken in large numbers. Thus, in time, Kamchatka and eastern Asia would be liberally supplied from hence with all kinds of vegetable and animal productions for the sustenance of life.

In 1812, ambitious Ivan Kuskov, second-in-command in Russian America, leapfrogged over the Oregon territory to erect just such a Russian settlement, on the very doorstep of Spanish America. A little north of San Francisco, on a plateau near Bodega Bay which he had scouted in 1809, Kuskov built his fortress.

Outside the stockade were granaries, workshops, and redwood huts for Aleut fishers and hunters. On the beach were a wharf, a tannery, and a shed for the skin-covered boats.

Fort Ross the Americans called it—the "Russian" or "Russ" fort. Its appearance in 1824 is described by young Lieutenant Otto von Kotzebue, who stopped there on his round-the-world voyage from St. Petersburg. The following selection is from Otto von Kotzebue's *A Voyage Round the World in the Years 1823 to 1826* (1830).

> From the summit of a high hill we at length to our great joy perceived beneath us the fortress of Ross, to which we descended by a tolerably convenient road. We spurred our tired horses and excited no small astonishment as we passed through the gate at a gallop. M. Von Schmidt, the governor of the establishment, received us in the kindest manner, fired some guns to greet our arrival on Russian-American ground and conducted us into his commodious and orderly mansion, built in the European fashion with thick beams. . . .
>
> The fortress is a quadrangle, palisaded with tall, thick beams and defended by two towers which

mount fifteen guns. The garrison consisted on my arrival of a hundred and thirty men, of whom a small number only were Russians, the rest Aleutians.

The Spaniards lived at first on the best terms with the new settlers and provided them with oxen, cows, horses and sheep; but when in process of time they began to remark that, notwithstanding the inferiority of soil and climate, the Russian establishment became more flourishing than theirs, envy and apprehension of future danger took possession of their minds. They then required that the settlement should be abandoned—asserted that their rights of dominion extended northward quite to the Icy Sea, and threatened to support their claims by force of arms.

The founder and then commander of the fortress of Ross, a man of penetration and one not easily frightened, gave a very decided answer. He had, he said, at the command of his superiors, settled in this region, which had not previously been in the possession of any other power, and over which, consequently, none had a right but the natives; that these latter had freely consented to his occupation of the land, and therefore that he would yield to no such unfounded pretension as that now advanced by the Spaniards, but should always be ready to resist force by force.

Perceiving that the Russians would not comply with their absurd requisitions, and considering that they were likely to be worsted in an appeal to arms, the Spaniards quietly gave up all further thought of hostilities and entered again into friendly communications with our people, since which the greatest unity has subsisted between the two nations.

The Spaniards often find Ross very serviceable to them. For instance, there is no such thing as a smith in all California; consequently the making and repairing of all manner of iron implements here is a great accommodation to them, and affords lucrative employment to the Russians. The dragoons who accompanied us had brought a number of old gunlocks to be repaired.

In order that the Russians might not extend their dominion to the northern shore of the Bay of San Francisco, the Spaniards immediately founded the missions of San Gabriel and San Francisco Solano. It is a great pity that we were not beforehand with them. The advantages of possessing this beautiful bay are incalculable, especially as we have no harbor but the bad one of Bodega or Port Romanzow.

The inhabitants of Ross live in the greatest concord with the Indians, who repair in considerable numbers to the fortress and work as day laborers for wages. At night they usually remain outside the palisades. They willingly give their daughters in marriage to Russians and Aleutians; and from these unions, ties of relationship have arisen which strengthen the good understanding between them.

The inhabitants of Ross have often penetrated singly far into the interior when engaged in the pursuit of deer or other game, and have passed whole nights among different Indian tribes, without ever having experienced any inconvenience. This the Spaniards dare not venture upon. The more striking the contrast between the two nations in their treatment of the savages, the more ardently must every friend to humanity rejoice on entering the Russian territory.

The Greek Church does not make converts by force. Free from fanaticism, she preaches only toleration and love. She does not even admit of persuasion, but trusts wholly to conviction for proselytes, who, when once they enter her communion, will always find her a loving mother. How different has been the conduct both of Catholic priests and Protestant missionaries!

The climate of Ross is mild. Réaumur's thermometer seldom falls to the freezing point; yet gardens cannot flourish on account of the frequent fogs. Some versts [half miles] farther inland beyond the injurious influence of the fog, plants of the warmest climates prosper surprisingly. Cucumbers of fifty pounds' weight, gourds of sixty-five, and other fruits in proportion are produced in them. Potatoes yield a hundred or two hundred fold, and . . . are an effectual security against famine.

The fortress is surrounded by wheat and barley fields which, on account of the fogs, are less productive than those of Santa Clara, but which still supply sufficient corn for the inhabitants of Ross. The Aleutians find their abode here so agreeable that, although very unwilling to leave their islands, they are seldom inclined to return to them. . . .

Ross is blessed with an abundance of the finest wood for building. The sea provides it with the most delicious fish; the land with an inexhaustible quantity of the best kinds of game; and, notwithstanding the want of a good harbor, the northern settlements might easily find in this a beautiful magazine for the supply of all their wants. . . .

The Indians of Ross are so much like those of the missions that they may well be supposed to belong to the same race, however different their language. They appear indeed by no means so stupid, and are much more cheerful and contented than at the missions, where a deep melancholy always clouds their faces, and their eyes are constantly fixed upon the ground; but this difference is only the natural result of the different treatment they experience.

They have no permanent residence, but wander about naked and, when not employed by the Russians as day laborers, follow no occupation but the chase. They are not difficult in the choice of their food, but consume the most disgusting things, not excepting all kinds of worms and insects. . . .

For the winter they lay up a provision of acorns and wild rye. The latter grows here very abundantly. . . . The Indians here have invented several games of chance; they are passionately fond of gaming, and often play away everything they possess. Should the blessing of civilization ever be extended to the rude inhabitants of these regions, the merit will be due to the Russian establishments, certainly not to the Spanish missions.

RUSSIAN RETREAT

For thirty years, Fort Ross stood on its 70-foot precipice overlooking the Pacific. The Russian chapel with its bulb-shaped dome, the Russian cannon, and the tall, bearded trappers brought a touch of St. Petersburg and the Kremlin to the New World.

Spaniards who had kindly provided grain for the starving Russians in 1813 continued their illegal trade with the northerners in spite of the governor. The Russians supplied them with iron, wood, and leather goods in return for food. Russians also tanned hides, fired brick, made rope from hemp grown at Fort Ross, and even built several small ships in the harbor on Bodega Bay. On festive occasions, the piano in the large officers' house tinkled, the rooms were bedecked with bright flowers grown in glass hot-houses, and the vodka flowed freely.

This tiny Russian island survived in the wilderness of California, but, after 1830, at an expense of 10,000 rubles a year to the Russian-American Company. It controlled barely enough land to feed itself. There was not enough pasture to raise cattle for beef for Sitka (New Archangel). Imported Russian laborers, who were legally serfs, had a way of escaping over the stockade to Spanish territory. Sea otter were becoming scarce, the Spaniards closed San Francisco Bay to the Aleut fishers, and the game near Fort Ross was exterminated.

Fort Ross not only failed to serve as a granary for Alaska, but was being steadily encircled by Spanish, later American, settlements. First Spain, then Mexico (after it gained its independence), refused to cede the territory to the Russians and ordered them to leave. A "Little Russia" stretching from Oregon south to include San Francisco and east to the Sierra Nevada never materialized.

Russia could have conquered the land without difficulty —except that it knew neither England nor the United States would permit that. President Monroe had spelled that out by his Doctrine (1823), which was backed by the British Navy. Mr. Monroe had stated that "the American continents . . . are henceforth not to be considered as subjects for future colonization by any European powers."

At last, in 1839, the Russian-American Company decided to cut its losses. Fort Ross was too distant from the rest of Russian America to be maintained—so it was put up for sale, as real estate. In 1841, it was purchased lock, stock, and barrel by the aggressive Swiss-American pioneer Johann Augustus Sutter. The price was $50,000.

The sale was symbolic. A new force had arrived in California, consisting of lanky, tough mountain men and Yankee mariners. Unlike the Russians, these Americans had come to stay.

4

Boston Clippers and Mountain Men

> We hurried on, filled with excitement, to escape entirely from the horrid region of inhospitable snow to the perpetual spring of the Sacramento.
> —John C. Fremont,
>   Report of the Exploring Expedition to Oregon and North California in the Years 1843–44

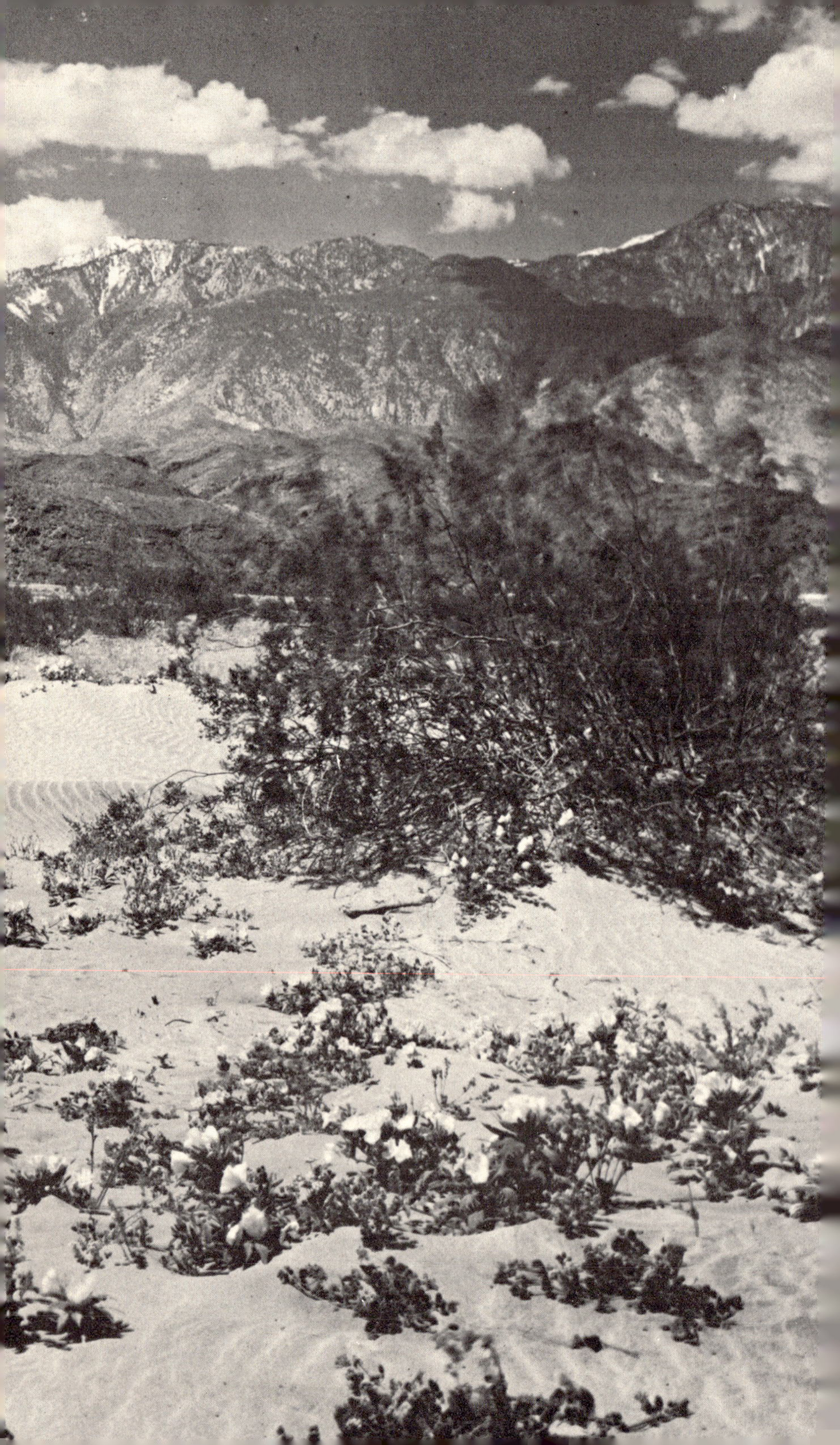

Richard Henry Dana

Jedediah Smith's arrival at San Gabriel Mission

REVOLUTION IN MEXICO

When Rezanov courted Concepción Argüello in 1806, California was part of the Spanish empire. Soon after that, however, a revolution against Spain began in Mexico. This struggle lasted until 1821, when a different flag was raised in California—the green, white, and red banner of the Mexican Republic.

In Europe, Napoleon was redrawing the map and shuffling thrones like a deck of cards. One of his discards was King Charles IV of Spain; in place of Charles IV he set his brother Joseph on the Spanish throne. The colonists in Mexico indignantly refused to recognize the usurper Joseph Bonaparte. They resolved to govern themselves until Charles IV returned to power.

But *how* would the colonists rule themselves? The only machinery of government was the bureaucracy controlled from Spain, now under Bonaparte. Unlike the Americans, whose Declaration of Independence they admired, the Spanish colonists had developed no legislatures of their own.

And *who* would rule? There were two factions suspicious of each other: the Spaniards recently arrived from the mother country, called Gachupines, and the Creoles, persons of Spanish descent born in Mexico. The Gachupines held the most important positions and were envied by the Creoles. (At the bottom of the social pyramid were the Indians—like the black slaves in the United States.)

When the viceroy of Mexico seemed to favor the

Creoles, the Gachupines took a fatal step. In 1808, they revolted against the viceroy—that is, against the legitimate government. The Gachupines seized power by a coup (sudden blow) under a *caudillo* (military leader or dictator). This kind of "election" became very popular in Spanish America. Soon a coup was being prepared against the Gachupines.

A stormy period followed, during which Californians remained loyal to Spain and perhaps wished that their land were nearer the North Pole. There was no civil war in California, but its inhabitants suffered, nevertheless because of the strife in Mexico. Soldiers and missionaries did not receive their pay. After 1808, few supply ships came up from Mexico. The people were more dependent than ever upon the missions for food and clothing. Officials were more willing to look the other way when Russian or American ships arrived and traded with the inhabitants.

One day in November, 1818, two privateers, commanded by a big, brutal Frenchman, Hippolyte de Bouchard, appeared and sacked Monterey. There were no other raids on California, but rumors flew about bloody battles in Mexico. Finally, in 1821, Colonel Agustín de Iturbide seized power and declared Mexico independent. California had no choice but to announce its allegiance to Iturbide, who soon promoted himself to emperor and then was overthrown.

A period of weak government followed, during which trade and immigration restrictions were relaxed. Yankees now not only traded with Californians but began to infiltrate and settle in their territory.

ACROSS THE DESERT

Resourceful Jedediah Smith, of New England descent, was the first Yankee to break through California's eastern barrier. In 1826, with a handful of followers in ragged buckskins, he made his way southwest from near the Great Salt Lake to Arizona, then across the desert to San Gabriel Mission, outside Los Angeles. The astonished friars received the Americans kindly and gave them food and lodging. But Governor José María Echeandía, at San Diego, threw Smith in jail.

Officials sent to California from the Mexican Republic did not welcome the Anglo-Saxons. California was still thinly populated and exposed to conquest. The governor freed Smith only on his promise to leave California and never return. Smith did eventually depart but not before he had explored the great Central Valley; then he came back and opened a trail from California to Oregon. Other American trappers heard of the riches in furs discovered by Smith and followed in his footsteps.

An adventurous Kentuckian, James O. Pattie, started southwest from the Missouri River with his father and a small band in 1824. They wandered across New Mexico and Arizona, losing one cache of furs to the Mexican governor at Santa Fe, who confiscated them. They buried another cache, after their pack animals were stampeded by Indians. Then they struggled to survive in the Colorado Desert. In 1828, they staggered into Santa Catalina Mission in Lower California—and, like Jedediah Smith, wound up in the San Diego *calabozo* (guardhouse).

The following selection, describing the crossing of the desert and the imprisonment, is from James O. Pattie's exciting *Personal Narrative* (1831).

> We started on the 26th, with our two [Indian] guides. . . . We struck off a south west course, which led in the direction of the snow covered mountain, which still loomed up in its brightness before us.
>
> Our guides made signs that we should arrive at the foot about midnight, though the distance appeared

to us to be too great to be travelled over in so short a time. We were yet to learn, that we should find no water, until we drank that of the melted snow. We perceived, however, that their travelling gait, worn as we were, was more rapid than ours.

We pushed on as fast as we could a league further, when we were impeded by a high hill in our way.... When we reached the top of it we were much exhausted, and began to be thirsty. We could then see the arid salt plain stretching all the way from the foot of this hill to the snow covered mountains.

We thought it inexpedient to enquire of our guides, if there was no water to be found between us and the mountain.... To know it to a certainty, would only tend to unnerve and dishearten us.... We found it best to encourage the little hope that remained, and hurried on through the drifted sand, in which we sank up to our ankles at every step.

The cloudless sun poured such a blaze upon it, that by the scorching of our feet, it might have seemed almost hot enough to roast eggs in. What with the fierce sun and the scorching sand, and our extreme fatigue, the air seemed soon to have extracted every particle of moisture from our bodies. In this condition we marched on until nearly the middle of the day....

A small shrubby tree stood in our way, affording a tolerable shade. We laid ourselves down to get a few minutes rest. The Indians sternly beckoned us to be up and onward, now for the first time clearly explaining to us, that there was no water until we reached the mountains in view....

We attempted to chew tobacco. It would raise no moisture. We took our bullets in our mouths, and moved them round to create a moisture, to relieve our parched throats. We had travelled but a little farther before our tongues had become so dry and swollen, that we could scarcely speak so as to be understood....

We marched on in company a few miles further. Two of our companions here gave out, and lay down under the shade of a bush. Their tongues were so swollen, and their eyes so sunk in their heads, that they were a spectacle to behold.... We never expected to see them again, and none of us had much hope of ever reaching the mountain, which still raised its white summit at a great distance from us.... The excessive and dazzling brightness of the sun's rays, so reflected in our eyes from the white sand that we were scarcely able to see our way before us.... However, we still kept moving onward....

[At night] we stopped, and made a large fire, that our companions, if yet living ... might see where we were.... We also fired some guns, which, to our great relief and pleasure, they answered by firing off theirs. We still repeated firing guns at intervals, until they came up with us.

They supposed that we had found water, which ... aroused them to the effort they had made. When they ... found that we had reached no water, they appeared to be angry and to complain that we had ... hindered their dying in peace....

As soon as there was light ... we started.... At about ten in the forenoon we arrived at the foot of a sand hill about a half a mile in height, and very steep. The side was composed of loose sand, which gave way under our feet.... At two in the afternoon we found a place that was neither so steep nor so high ... but my father and another of our company ... gave out below.... [My father] insisted that I should go on with the rest, and if I found any water near at hand, that I should return with my powder horn full. . . .

Having descended this hill, we ascended another of the same wearying ascent, and sandy character. . . . We toiled on to the top of it. The Eternal Power . . . had had mercy upon us! Imagine my joy at seeing a clear, beautiful running stream of water, just below us at the foot of the hill! . . . We all ran down to it, and fell to drinking. In a few moments nothing was to be heard among us but vomiting and groaning. . . . We had overcharged our parched stomachs with this cold snow water. . . .

I emptied my powder horn of its contents, filled it with water, and accompanied by one companion, who had also filled his powder horn, I returned towards my father and Mr. Slover. . . . We found them . . . stretched on the sand at full length . . . fast asleep. . . . Their lips were black, and their parched mouths wide open. . . .

I ran in a fright to my father, thinking him . . . really dead. But he easily awakened, and drank the refreshing water. My companion at the same time bestowed his horn of water upon Mr. Slover. In . . . an hour they were both able to climb the hill, and some time before dark we rejoined the remainder of our company.

The Americans reached Santa Catalina Mission in Lower California—and were clapped in jail! After a week, they were dispatched to San Diego and another jail, described by James O. Pattie below. The selection is from Pattie's *Personal Narrative* (1831).

Next day the kind serjeant brought my dinner again, though from anxiety and growing indisposition I was unable to eat. At night he came again with my supper, and to my surprise accompanied by his sister, a young lady of great personal beauty. Her first inquiry was that of a kind and affectionate nature, and concerned my father. She enquired about my age, and all the circumstances that induced me to leave my country?

I took leave to intimate in my answer, my extreme anxiety to see my relatives, and return to my country, and in particular, that it was like depriving me of life, in this strange land, and in prison, to separate me from my old and infirm father.

She assured me that she would pray for our salvation, and attempt to intercede with the general in our behalf, and that while we remained in prison, she would allow us to suffer nothing. . . . She then wished me a good night, and departed. I know not what is the influence of the ministration of a kind spirit, like hers, but this night my sleep was sound and dreamless.

She frequently repeated these kind visits, and redeemed to the letter all her pledges of kindness. For I suffered for nothing in regard to food or drink. A bed was provided for me, and even a change of clothing. This undeviating kindness greatly endeared her to me.

About this time, Captain John Bradshaw, of the ship *Franklin,* and Rufus Perkins, his supercargo, asked leave of the general, to come and visit us. The general denied them. But Captain Bradshaw, like a true hearted American, disregarded the little brief authority of this miserable republican despot and . . . came to see me without leave. When I spoke to him about our buried furs, he asked me about the chances and the means we had to bring them in? And whether we were disposed to make the effort, and if we succeeded, to sell them to him?

The prisoners . . . one and all assured him, that nothing would give them more pleasure. He assured us, that he would leave nothing in his power undone, in making efforts to deliver us from our confinement.

Captain Bradshaw obtained a few hours' liberty for James Pattie, on the plea that he needed Pattie's services as an interpreter. The two went to an old Spanish captain in charge of arms, whom Bradshaw knew, and this captain agreed to speak to the general in Pattie's behalf and went off to do so.

During this interval, we walked to my father's cell, and I had the satisfaction of speaking with him through the grates. He asked me if I had been visited by a beautiful young lady? When I assented, he replied, that this charming young woman, as a ministering angel, had also visited his cell with every sort of kindness and relief, which she had extended to each one of our companions. I had the satisfaction, afterwards, of speaking with each one of our companions. . . . From these visits I returned to the office of the captain of arms.
We found him waiting with the most painful intelligence [news]. Nothing could move the general, to allow us to go out and bring in our furs. . . . I took my leave of him, returning to my dreary prison, less buoyant and more completely desponding of my liberty than ever.

CLIPPERS AROUND CAPE HORN

Rough, wandering trappers were not welcome in California. But clipper ships which battled the gales around Cape Horn to bring manufactured goods to the West Coast were better received. The Mexican government, more lenient than Spain had been, permitted ships to obtain a trading license at Monterey. Then the "Boston ship" would sail slowly down the coast, making frequent stops.

It would anchor just beyond the surf and send its boat in to fetch the eager rancheros and their wives, who would shop excitedly among the shoes, satins, velvets, toys, saddles, spurs, tools, furniture, etc. piled in its hold.

In return for their goods, the shrewd Yankees took cattle hides, sometimes packing 30,000 hides in one ship. They carried the hides to New England, where they were made into leather goods, which then returned to California—at a handsome profit to the traders. Shoes which cost $3 in Boston brought $30 in California. The merchants also collected tallow, melted down from the fat of slaughtered cattle, and sea otter and beaver pelts. Their business, after a quarter of a century, was valued at $20,000,000.

A number of merchants and shore-based agents, as well as deserters from the ships, remained in California. "Leaving their consciences at Cape Horn," they married *señoritas*, embraced the Catholic faith, and became Mexican citizens.

One Yankee who did not stay, but who observed the Californians keenly, was a young Harvard student, Richard Henry Dana. In 1833, Dana had a bad case of measles which left his eyes temporarily too weak for reading. So in 1834 he took a work vacation and signed on the brig *Pilgrim* for a voyage to California.

Young Dana was intelligent, sensitive, and courageous. He would be a hero to his fellow students after he returned from his two-year voyage. And he would develop a deep sympathy for the downtrodden because of the injustices he saw done to his comrades, the common sailors. Later, as a lawyer, he would defend them in court against their captains; still later, he would assist in the underground railroad by which slaves escaped from the South to Canada. Lincoln made Dana United States District Attorney for Massachusetts.

In 1840, Dana published his account of his voyage, *Two Years Before the Mast,* which immediately became a classic. The following selection, describing the rounding of Cape Horn, anchoring in the Santa Barbara roadstead, and loading hides on a ship, is from Dana's *Two Years Before the Mast* (1840).

During the first part of this day (Wednesday) the wind was light, but after noon it came on fresh, and we furled the royals. We still kept the studding-sails out, and the captain said he should go round with them, if he could. Just before eight o'clock (then about sundown in that latitude) the cry of "All hands ahoy!" was sounded down the fore scuttle and the after hatchway, and hurrying upon deck, we found a large black cloud rolling on toward us from the south-west, and blackening the whole heavens.

"Here comes Cape Horn!" said the chief mate; and we had hardly time to haul down and clew up, before it was upon us. In a few moments, a heavier sea was raised than I had ever seen before, and as it was directly ahead, the little brig, which was no better than a bathing machine, plunged into it, and all the forward part of her was under water; the sea pouring in through the bow-ports and hawse-hole and over the knightheads, threatening to wash everything overboard. In the lee scuppers it was up to a man's waist.

We sprang aloft and double reefed the topsail, and furled all the other sails, and made all snug. But this would not do; the brig was laboring and straining against the head sea, and the gale was growing worse and worse. At the same time sleet and hail were driving with all fury against us.

We clewed down, and hauled out the reef-tackles

again, and close-reefed the fore-topsail, and furled the main, and hove her to on the starboard tack. Here was an end to our fine prospects. We made up our minds to head winds and cold weather. . . .

Throughout the night it stormed violently—rain, hail, snow, and sleet beating the vessel—the wind continuing ahead, and the sea running high. At daybreak (about three, A.M.) the deck was covered with snow. The captain sent up the steward with a glass of grog to each of the watch; and all the time that we were off the Cape, grog was given to the morning watch, and to all hands whenever we reefed topsails.

The clouds cleared away at sunrise, and the wind becoming more fair, we again made sail and stood nearly up to our course.

After rounding the Cape and stopping at the island of Juan Fernández, off Chile, to take on water, the *Pilgrim* sailed on northward.

We continued sailing along in the beautiful temperate climate of the Pacific. The Pacific well deserves its name, for except in the southern part, at Cape Horn, and in the western parts, near the China and Indian oceans, it has few storms, and is never either extremely hot or cold. Between the tropics there is a slight haziness, like a thin gauze, drawn over the sun, which . . . tempers the heat. . . .

I shall never forget the impression which our first landing on the beach of California made upon me. The sun had just gone down; it was getting dusky; the damp night wind was beginning to blow, and the heavy swell of the Pacific was setting in, and breaking in loud and high "combers" upon the beach. We lay on our oars in the swell, just outside of the surf, waiting for a good chance to run in, when a boat, which had put off from the *Ayacucho* just after us, came alongside of us, with a crew of dusky Sandwich Islanders, talking and hallooing in their outlandish tongue. They knew that we were novices in this kind of boating, and waited to see us go in.

The second mate, however, who steered our boat, determined to have the advantage of their experience, and would not go in first. Finding, at length, how matters stood, they gave a shout, and taking advantage of a great comber which came swelling in, rearing its head, and lifting up the stern of our boat nearly perpendicular, and again dropping it in the trough, they gave three or four long and strong pulls, and went in on top of the great wave, throwing their oars overboard, and as far from the boat as they could throw them, and jumping out the instant that the boat touched the beach, and then seizing hold of her and running her up high and dry upon the sand.

We saw, at once, how it was to be done. . . . We pulled strongly in, and as soon as we felt that the sea had got hold of us and was carrying us in with the speed of a racehorse, we threw the oars as far from the boat as we could, and took hold of the gunwale, ready to spring out and seize her when she struck, the officer using his utmost strength to keep her stern on. We were shot up upon the beach like an arrow from a bow, and seizing the boat, ran her up high and dry, and soon picked up our oars, and stood by her, ready for the captain to come down.

Finding that the captain did not come immediately, we put our oars in the boat, and leaving one to watch it, walked about the beach to see what we could, of the place. The beach is nearly a mile in length between the two points, and of smooth sand. . . .

The Sandwich Islanders, in the mean time, had turned their boat round, and ran her down into the water, and were loading her with hides and tallow. As this was the work in which we were soon to be engaged, we looked on with some curiosity. They ran the boat into the water so far that every large sea might float her, and two of them, with their trowsers rolled up, stood by the bows, one on each side, keeping her in her right position. This was hard work; for beside the force they had to use upon the boat, the large seas nearly took them off their legs.

The others were running from the boat to the bank, upon which, out of the reach of the water, was a pile of dry bullocks' hides, doubled lengthwise in the middle, and nearly as stiff as boards. These they took upon their heads, one or two at a time, and carried down to the boat, where one of their number, stowed them away. They were obliged to carry them on their heads, to keep them out of the water, and we observed that they had on thick woolen caps.

"Look here, Bill, and see what you're coming to!" said one of our men to another who stood by the boat.

"Well, D——," said the second mate to me, "this does not look much like Cambridge college, does it? This is what I call *'head work.'*" To tell the truth it did not look very encouraging.

YANKEE SUPERMARKET

Once anchored in California waters, a Boston ship would turn itself into a bargain basement for eager shoppers. In the following passage Richard Henry Dana describes a lively sale on the *Pilgrim*—and also reveals some Anglo-Saxon prejudice toward the impoverished, peaceful Spanish-speaking people of California. The selection is from Dana's *Two Years Before the Mast* (1840).

The next day, the cargo having been entered in due form [at Monterey], we began trading. The trade-room was fitted up in the steerage, and furnished out with the lighter goods, and with specimens of the rest of the cargo; and M——, a young man who came out from Boston with us, before the mast, was taken out of the forecastle, and made supercargo's clerk. . . .

For a week or ten days all was life on board. The people came off to look and to buy—men, women, and children; and we were continually going in the boats, carrying goods and passengers,—for they have no boats of their own. Everything must dress itself and come aboard and see the new vessel, if it were only to buy a paper of pins. The agent and his clerk managed the sales, while we were busy in the hold or in the boats.

Our cargo was an assorted one; that is, it consisted of everything under the sun. We had spirits of all kinds, (sold by the cask,) teas, coffee, sugars, spices, raisins, molasses, hardware, crockery-ware, tinware, cutlery, clothing of all kinds, boots and shoes from Lynn, calicoes and cottons from Lowell, crepes, silks; also shawls, scarfs, necklaces, jewelry, and combs for the ladies; furniture; and in fact, everything that can be imagined, from Chinese fire-works to English cart-wheels—of which we had a dozen pairs with their iron rims on.

The Californians are an idle, thriftless people and can make nothing for themselves. The country abounds in grapes, yet they buy bad wines made in Boston and brought round by us, at an immense price, and retail it among themselves at a *real* (12½ cents) by the small wine-glass. Their hides, too, which they value at two dollars in money, they give for something which costs seventy-five cents in Boston; and buy shoes (like as not, made of their own hides, and which have been carried twice around Cape Horn) at three or four dollars, and "chicken-skin" boots at fifteen dollars apiece. Things sell, on an average, at an advance of nearly three hundred per cent upon the Boston prices. . . .

This kind of business was new to us, and we liked it very well, for a few days, though we were hard at work every minute from daylight to dark; and sometimes even later.

UNDER THE MEXICAN FLAG

California in the 1830's was changing. More mountain men with their long rifles and short tempers were settling in its brown hills. The missions were falling into ruins, their fields overgrown with weeds, their red-tiled churches in need of repair.

In 1833 the Mexican government had given the mission lands back to the Indians. But many Indians were unwilling and unprepared to be "liberated." They sold their lands to greedy rancheros for a few bottles of whiskey. Corrupt administrators seized some of the lands for themselves. Enterprising white neighbors stole herds of cattle from the mission fields.

Richard Henry Dana, with his sharp Yankee eyes, observed these changes. In the following passage he describes the decline of the missions and the growing political instability. The selection is from Dana's *Two Years Before the Mast* (1840).

Ever since the independence of Mexico, the missions have been going down; until, at last, a law was passed, stripping them of all their possessions, and confining the priests to their spiritual duties; and at the same time declaring all the Indians free and independent *Rancheros*. The change in the condition of the Indians was, as may be supposed, only nominal; they are virtually slaves, as much as they ever were.

But in the missions, the change was complete. The priests have now no power, except in their religious character, and the great possessions of the missions are given over to be preyed upon by the harpies of the civil power, who are sent there in the capacity of *administradores*, to settle up the concerns; and who usually end, in a few years, by making themselves fortunes, and leaving their stewardships worse than they found them.

The dynasty of the priests was much more acceptable to the people of the country, and indeed, to every one concerned with the country, by trade or otherwise, than that of the *administradores*. The priests were attached perpetually to one mission, and felt the necessity of keeping up its credit. Accordingly, their debts were regularly paid, and the people were, in the main, well treated, and attached to those who had spent their whole lives among them. But the *administradores* are strangers sent from Mexico, having no interest in the country; not identified in any way with their charge, and, for the most part, men of desperate fortunes—broken down politicians and soldiers—whose only object is to retrieve their condition in as short a time as possible. . . .

Revolutions are matters of constant occurrence in California. They are got up by men who are at the foot of the ladder and in desperate circumstances, just as a new political party is started by such men in our own country. The only object, of course, is the loaves and fishes; and instead of caucusing, paragraphing, libelling, feasting, promising, and lying, as with us, they take muskets and bayonets, and seizing upon the presidio and customhouse, divide the spoils, and declare a new dynasty.

As for justice, they know no law but will and fear. A Yankee, who had been naturalized, and become a Catholic, and had married in the country, was sitting in his house at the Pueblo de los Angeles, with his wife and children, when a Spaniard, with whom he had had a difficulty, entered the house, and stabbed him to the heart before them all. The murderer was seized by some Yankees who had settled there, and kept in confinement until a statement of the whole affair could be sent to the governor-general.

He refused to do anything about it, and the countrymen of the murdered man, seeing no prospect of justice being administered, made known that if nothing was done, they should try the man themselves. It chanced that, at this time, there was a company of forty trappers and hunters from Kentucky, with their rifles, who had made their head-quarters at the Pueblo; and these, together with the Americans and Englishmen in the place, who were between twenty and thirty in number, took possession of the town, and waiting a reasonable time, proceeded to try the man according to the forms in their own country.

A judge and jury were appointed, and he was tried, convicted, sentenced to be shot, and carried out before the town, with his eyes blindfolded. The names of all the men were then put into a hat and each one pledging himself to perform his duty, twelve names were drawn out, and the men took their stations with their rifles, and, firing at the word, laid him dead. He was decently buried, and the place was restored quietly to the proper authorities.

A general, with titles enough for an hidalgo, was at San Gabriel, and issued a proclamation as long as the fore-top-bowline, threatening destruction to the rebels, but never stirred from his fort; for forty Kentucky hunters, with their rifles, were a match for a whole regiment of hungry, drawling, lazy half-breeds. This affair happened while we were at San Pedro, (the port of the Pueblo,) and we had all the particulars directly from those who were on the spot.

FRÉMONT MAPS THE WAY

In the 1840's Yankee seamen, salesmen, and trappers were followed into California by Yankee settlers. In 1841, under John Bidwell, the first party set out from Independence, Missouri, in their covered wagons, headed for the Pacific coast.

These pioneers desperately needed to know reliable trails west. Trappers' reports were at first all they had; these were by word of mouth and sometimes contradicted each other. But soon accurate United States government surveys became available.

In 1842 a government expedition led by the dashing Army engineer John C. Frémont had mapped the route to Oregon. The next year, Frémont explored again in the northwest; in December, 1843, he found himself, with a small party, almost snowbound on the eastern slope of the Sierra Nevada below Lake Tahoe. With the impulsiveness that got him both into and out of trouble all his life, the bronzed, black-bearded Frémont decided to go on, up over the 9,300-foot range blanketed with 15 feet of snow.

He had to abandon his twelve-pound brass howitzer, but on February 20, 1844, he and his men stumbled blindly against the icy blast, over the divide. Far below, they glimpsed the green valleys and soft blue skies of California. Although he was not the discoverer of this route,

Frémont would now blaze the trail with his maps, distributed all over the United States. Thousands would follow his directions to the promised land.

The following selection, describing Frémont's crossing into California, is from John Charles Frémont, *Report of the Exploring Expedition to Oregon and North California in the Years 1843-44* (1845).

February 14th. With Mr. Preuss, I ascended today the highest peak near us, from which we had a beautiful view of a mountain lake at our feet, about fifteen miles in length. . . . The valley was half hidden in mist. . . . Snow could be distinguished on the higher parts of the coast mountains; eastward, as far as the eye could extend, it ranged over a terrible mass of broken snowy mountains, fading off blue in the distance.

The rock composing the summit consists of a very coarse dark volcanic conglomerate; the lower parts appeared to be of a slaty structure. The highest trees were a few scattering cedars and aspens. From the immediate foot of the peak, we were two hours in reaching the summit, and one hour and a quarter in descending.

The day had been very bright, still, and clear, and spring seems to be advancing rapidly. While the sun is in the sky, the snow melts rapidly, and gushing springs cover the face of the mountain in all the exposed places; but their surface freezes instantly with the disappearance of the sun.

I obtained tonight some observations; and the result from these, and others made during our stay, gives for the latitude 38° 41' 57", longitude 120° 25' 57". . . .

February 16th. . . . We started again early in the morning. The creek acquired a regular breadth of about twenty feet, and we soon began to hear the rushing of the water below the icy surface, over which we traveled to avoid the snow; a few miles below we broke through where the water was several feet deep, and halted to make a fire and dry our clothes. We continued a few miles farther, walking being very laborious without snowshoes.

I was now perfectly satisfied that we had struck the stream on which Mr. Sutter lived; and turning about, made a hard push and reached the camp at dark. . . .

On the afternoon of . . . February 20, 1844, we encamped with the animals and all the matériel . . . on the summit of the pass in the dividing ridge. . . . The temperature of boiling water gave for the elevation of the encampment nine thousand three hundred and thirty-eight feet above the sea. This was two thousand feet higher than the South Pass in the Rocky Mountains. . . . Latitude 38° 44′; longitude 120° 28′. Thus this pass in the Sierra Nevada, which so well deserves its name of Snowy Mountain, is eleven degrees west, and about four degrees south, of the South Pass.

February 21st. We now considered ourselves victorious over the mountain; having only the descent before us, and the valley under our eyes, we felt strong hope that we should force our way down.

SUTTER'S FORT

After crossing the Sierra Nevada divide, Frémont led his men toward Sutter's Fort. Sutter's Fort, also called New Helvetia (New Switzerland), was a true fortress on the Sacramento River. It had adobe walls 18 feet high and 3 feet thick, protected by twelve cannon. Within were workshops and storage buildings, while outside, Indians worked in broad, irrigated wheat fields or tended cattle in green pastures. It was like a medieval barony set down in the California wilderness.

Johann Augustus Sutter was a blond, blue-eyed Swiss emigrant with an erect military bearing. In 1839 this "dreamer with a gifted tongue" had obtained permission from Mexican authorities to develop 50,000 acres near the junction of the Sacramento and American rivers. The officials hoped to encourage settlement of the interior of California as a bulwark against foreign penetration. In 1840, with the help of the American merchant William Heath Davis, Sutter chose his site and equipped his fort in part with gear from Russian Fort Ross.

But then Sutter began to help American immigrants arriving in California by the northern route—to the annoyance of the officials. The last thing they had desired was to set up a "welcome wagon" for Anglo-Saxons. The officials could do little but fume, however; Sutter's isolation, arms, and loyal Indians—whom he won over by fair treatment—made him practically independent.

The following selection, describing Frémont's arrival in this friendly haven, is from Frémont's *Report of the Exploring Expedition to Oregon and North California in the Years 1843–44* (1845).

March 6, 1844. . . . We continued on our road through the same surpassingly beautiful country, entirely unequaled for the pasturage of stock by anything we had ever seen. Our horses had now become so strong that they were able to carry us, and we traveled rapidly—over four miles an hour; four of us riding every alternate hour.

Every few hundred yards we came upon a little band of deer; but we were too eager to reach the settlement . . . to halt for any other than a passing shot. In a few hours we reached a large fork, the northern branch of the [American] river, and equal in size to that which we had descended. Together they formed a beautiful stream, 60 to 100 yards wide; which at first . . . we took to be the Sacramento [River].

We continued down the right bank of the river, traveling for a while over a wooded upland, where we had the delight to discover tracks of cattle. To the southwest was visible a black column of smoke, which we had frequently noticed in descending, arising from the fires we had seen from the top of the Sierra [Nevada]. From the upland we descended into broad groves on the river. . . .

Following the tracks of the horses and cattle in search of people, we discovered a small village of Indians. Some of these had on shirts of civilized manufacture, but were otherwise naked, and we could understand nothing from them; they appeared entirely astonished at seeing us.

We made an acorn meal at noon, and hurried on, the valley being gay with flowers, and some of the banks being absolutely golden with the California poppy (*Eschscholtzia crocea*). Here the grass was smooth and green, and the groves very open, the large oaks throwing a broad shade among sunny spots.

Shortly afterward we gave a shout at the appearance on a little bluff of a neatly built adobe house with glass windows. We rode up, but, to our disappointment, found only Indians. There was no appearance of cultivation, and we could see no cattle, and we supposed the place had been abandoned.

We now pressed on more eagerly than ever; the river swept round in a large bend to the right, the hills lowered down entirely; and, gradually entering a broad valley, we came unexpectedly into a large Indian village, where the people looked clean, and wore cotton shirts and various other articles of dress.

They immediately crowded around us, and we had

the inexpressible delight to find one who spoke a little indifferent Spanish, but who at first confounded us by saying there were no whites in the country; but just then a well-dressed Indian came up, and made his salutations in very well spoken Spanish.

In answer to our inquiries he informed us that we were upon the Río de los Americanos (the River of the Americans), and that it joined the Sacramento River about ten miles below. Never did a name sound more sweetly! We felt ourselves among our countrymen; for the name of "American," in these distant parts, is applied to the citizens of the United States.

To our eager inquiries he answered, "I am a vaquero (cowherd) in the service of Captain Sutter, and the people of this *rancheria* work for him." Our evident satisfaction made him communicative, and he went on to say that Captain Sutter was a very rich man, and always glad to see his country people. We asked for his house. He answered that it was just over the hill before us and offered . . . to take his horse and conduct us to it.

We readily accepted his civil offer. In a short distance we came in sight of the fort. . . . We forded the river; and in a few miles were met a short distance from the fort by Captain Sutter himself. He gave us a most frank and cordial reception—conducted us immediately to his residence—and under his hospitable roof we had a night of rest, enjoyment, and refreshment. . . .

Captain Sutter emigrated to this country from the western part of Missouri in 1838–39, and formed the first settlement in the valley on a large grant of land which he obtained from the Mexican Government. He had, at first, some trouble with the Indians; but by the occasional exercise of well-timed authority, he has succeeded in converting them into a peaceable and industrious people.

The ditches around his extensive wheat fields; the making of the sun-dried bricks of which his fort is constructed; the plowing, harrowing, and other agricultural operations, are entirely the work of these Indians, for which they receive a very moderate compensation—principally in shirts, blankets, and other articles of clothing....

There were at this time a number of girls at the fort, in training for a future woolen factory; but they were now all busily engaged in constantly watering the gardens.... The occasional dryness of some seasons I understood to be the only complaint of the settlers in this fertile valley.... Mr. Sutter was about making arrangements to irrigate his lands by means of the Río de los Americanos. He had this year sown.... three hundred fanegas [480 bushels] of wheat.

A few years since the neighboring Russian establishment of Ross, being about to withdraw from the country, sold to him a large number of stock, with agricultural and other stores, with a number of pieces of artillery, and other munitions of war; for these a regular yearly payment is made in grain.

The fort [Sutter's Fort] is a quadrangular adobe structure, mounting twelve pieces of artillery (two of them brass), and capable of admitting a garrison of a thousand men; this, at present, consists of forty Indians, in uniform—one of whom was always found on duty at the gate. As might naturally be expected, the pieces are not in very good order.

The whites in the employment of Captain Sutter, American, French, and German, amount, perhaps, to thirty men. The inner wall is formed into buildings comprising the common quarters, with a blacksmith's and other workshops; the dwelling house, with a large distillery house, and other buildings, occupying more the center of the area.

It is built upon a pondlike stream, at times a running creek communicating with the Río de los Americanos, which enters the Sacramento about two miles below. The latter is here a noble river, about three hundred yards broad, deep and tranquil, with several fathoms of water in the channel, and its banks continuously timbered. There were two vessels belonging to Captain Sutter at anchor near the landing—one a large two-masted lighter, and the other a schooner, which was shortly to proceed on a voyage to Fort Vancouver for a cargo of goods.

WESTWARD BOUND

So now not the Russians but the Americans were coming to California. By the mid-1840's 7,000 of them had crossed the prairies and mountains to the Pacific coast. Although only 1,500 of these had gone to California, more and more emigrants were turning south.

They departed from picturesque Independence, Missouri, which is described in the following selection, from J. Quinn Thornton's *The California Tragedy* (1849).

> The town of Independence was at this time a great Babel upon the border of the wilderness. Here might be seen the African slave with his shining black face, driving his six-horse team of blood-red bays, and swaying from side to side as he sat upon the saddle and listened to the incessant tinkling of the bells. In one street, just driving out of town, was an emigrant, who, having completed all his preparations, was about

entering upon the great prairie wilderness; whistling as though his mouth had been made for nothing else....

Here might be seen the indolent dark-skinned Spaniard smoking a cigar as he leans against the sunny side of a house. He wears a sharp conical hat with a red band; a blue roundabout, with little brass buttons; his duck pantaloons are open at the side as high as the knee....

Santa Fe wagons were coming in, having attached to them eight or ten mules, some driven by Spaniards, some by Americans resembling Indians, some by negroes.... The dilapidated and muddy condition of their wagons, and wagon-sheets, and the sore backs of their mules, all giving evidence of the length and toil of the journey.

Welcomed by the hospitable Sutter, the Americans were settling in the sunny valleys of the Sacramento and American rivers. Here, from time to time, to the dismay of the Mexican officials, the Stars and Stripes was raised on California soil.

5

The Stars and Stripes

> *Henceforward California will be a portion of the United States, and its peaceful inhabitants will enjoy the same rights and privileges as the citizens of any other portion of that territory.*
> —Commodore John D. Sloat, U.S. Navy, Proclamation, 1846

General Stephen W. Kearny

Commodore "Fighting Bob" Stockton

General Mariano Vallejo

PLANNING AN ATTACK

"The banner of the stars," as the Mexicans called our flag, was raised not only in California. In 1845 Texas became part of the United States.

"Go West, young man, go West," admonished Horace Greeley, the popular editor of the New York *Tribune.* "Manifest destiny" demanded that Americans fill the continent, from sea to shining sea. And backwoodsmen in buckskins, farmers, Mormons, clerks were heeding this advice. Covered wagons, like ships sailing in line, breasted the prairies.

But if "manifest destiny" decreed that California and the southwest become ours, what did it decree for the followers of Cabrillo and Father Serra, who already occupied the land? What did it promise the Indians, converted and unconverted?

In 1845 the United States government offered Mexico $5,000,000 for New Mexico and said, "Money would be no object," if Mexico would cede California. Mexico indignantly replied that California was not for sale. When the United States annexed Texas after its successful revolt of 1836, Mexicans were resentful. They suspected the "colossus of the north" of scheming to conquer all North America. They would have liked to get Texas back; they did not accept the Rio Grande as their northern boundary.

In the tense summer of 1845, just after the annexation of Texas, the United States government made "contingency plans" for a war with Mexico. The following selection shows how these plans would affect California. It is from a revealing letter sent by George Bancroft, Secretary of the Navy, to Commodore John D. Sloat, commander of the Pacific fleet (from Exec. Doc., No. 60, 30th Congress, 1st Session).

>Your attention is still particularly directed to the present aspect of the relations between this country and Mexico. It is the earnest desire of the President [Polk] to pursue the policy of peace; and he is anxious that you, and every part of your squadron, should be assiduously careful to avoid any act which could be construed as an act of aggression.
>
>Should Mexico, however, be resolutely bent on hostilities, you will be mindful to protect the persons and interests of citizens of the United States near your station; and, should you ascertain beyond a doubt that the Mexican government has declared war against us, you will at once employ the force under your command to the best advantage. The Mexican ports on the Pacific are said to be open and defenceless. If you ascertain with certainty that Mexico has declared war against the United States, you will at once possess yourself of the port of San Francisco, and blockade or occupy such other ports as your force may permit.
>
>Yet, even if you should find yourself called upon by the certainty of an express declaration of war against the United States to occupy San Francisco and other Mexican ports, you will be careful to preserve, if possible, the most friendly relations with the inhabitants; and, where you can do so, you will encourage them to adopt a course of neutrality.

THE BEAR FLAG REVOLT

Through the hills behind San Francisco roamed rough, leather-shirted American trappers who might not wait for an official declaration of war. They feared that some "European power"—England or France—might seize California first.

They had been excited by Frémont's mysterious visit to Sutter's Fort in 1845. Now, a year later, the lithe "Pathfinder" in his deerskin shirt, blue army trousers, and cotton handkerchief bound around his head returned on another "exploring" expedition. At once Spanish-speaking *Californios* suspected, and Americans hoped, that Frémont came as an agent to stir up revolution.

Frémont actually raised the American flag at his camp overlooking the Salinas Valley. Only reluctantly, at the urgent request of the American consul, Thomas Larkin, did Frémont withdraw toward Oregon. Rumors about his having recommended a "neutral conquest" of California by American settlers flew from ranch to ranch.

Then someone forged a proclamation in the name of the Mexican commandant, José Castro. By it, Americans were ordered out of the province. Immediately, the Bear Flag Revolt broke out. This was a revolt of a handful of bold Americans aiming to make California independent.

Early in June, 1846, Ezekiel Merritt led them in seizing a drove of horses from *vaqueros* near Sutter's Fort. On June 14, William Ide and thirty-one followers captured General Mariano Vallejo—who had been friendly to the Americans—in his own home, in Sonoma.

This exploit of the footloose hunters and trappers has been turned into a romantic legend. However, in the selection below, Hubert Howe Bancroft, California's most distinguished historian, gives a realistic account of the event. The selection is from Hubert Howe Bancroft's *Works*, Volume XXII.

In narratives of the time, and later, it was customary to magnify the exploit of June 14th [1846], by speaking of Sonoma as a Californian stronghold . . . taken by surprise, or even by a "gallant charge" without shedding of blood. . . .

There was, however, no garrison at Sonoma. The soldiers . . . there had been discharged some years before. . . . Some of the citizens even were absent from the town, and there was no thought of even posting a sentinel. It is true, there remained as relics of the old military regime nine small cannon, a few of them still mounted, and over 200 muskets in the *cuartel* [barracks]. . . . A more peaceful burg than this stronghold of the Frontera del Norte [Frontier of the North] on that Sunday morning it would be difficult to find.

At daybreak [Colonel] Vallejo [founder and landlord of Sonoma] was aroused by a noise, and on looking out saw that his house was surrounded by armed men. . . . Says [an eyewitness]: "Almost the whole party was dressed in leather hunting shirts, many of them very greasy; taking the whole party together, they were about as rough a looking set of men as one could well imagine." . . .

Vallejo's wife was even more alarmed than her husband, whom she begged to escape by a back door, but who, deeming such a course undignified as well as impracticable, hastily dressed, ordered the front door opened, and met the intruders as they entered. . . .

Early in the ensuing negotiations between prisoners and [the American] filibusters, it became apparent that the latter had neither acknowledged leader nor regular plan of operations beyond the seizure of government property and of the officers. . . . All seemed to agree, however, that they were acting under Frémont's orders, and this to the prisoners was the most assuring feature in the case. Vallejo had for some time favored the annexation of California to the United States. . . .

Accordingly . . . he submitted to arrest, gave up keys to public property, and entered upon negotiations with a view to obtain guaranties of protection for non-combatants. The guaranties sought were . . . signed by the respective parties [but not observed by the rank-and-file filibusters]. . . .

For four or five days . . . several weighty matters of state were disposed of by these soi-disant [so-called] founders of a republic. . . . The need of a banner was . . . suggested. The insurgents had no right to unfurl the stars and stripes, as many of them would doubtless have preferred to do; yet any flag devised by Americans must needs have at least a star and a stripe; and the appropriateness of a lone star could not fail to suggest itself to men familiar with the history of Texas. . . .

A simple copy would not, however, suffice, and an additional emblem was required. Somebody proposed the grizzly bear, an animal . . . [with a] reputation for "strength and unyielding resistance". . . . For materials they took . . . a piece of common unbleached cotton cloth . . . somewhat less than a yard in width and five feet long, and some strips of red flannel about four inches wide.

The flannel, the stripe of the flag, . . . was sewn to the bottom of the cotton. In the upper left-hand corner of the white field was outlined in ink, and filled in with red paint, an irregular five-pointed star. . . . Just to the right of the star, and facing it, was painted in like manner what was intended for a bear . . . though it has been pronounced more like a hog by experts. . . . Under the two emblems was rudely lettered in black ink CALIFORNIA REPUBLIC. Such was the famous Bear Flag, which has given a name to the revolution, and which caused the insurgents to be known to the natives as Osos [Bears]. . . .

The leaders . . . were all mere filibusters, and were entitled to none of the sympathy or honor which the world accords to revolutionists who struggle against oppression.

LANDING AT SAN FRANCISCO

On May 31, while off the coast of Mexico, Commodore John D. Sloat learned that fighting had started between American and Mexican forces along the Rio Grande. He took the Pacific fleet north to California and on July 7, 1846, landed and raised the American flag over Monterey. He then ordered Captain John B. Montgomery, of the *Portsmouth*, to occupy Yerba Buena (San Francisco).

With Montgomery went Joseph T. Downey, a young sailor from Louisiana who spoke of himself as "a wild, harum-scarum blade." Downey described the festive "capture" of Yerba Buena in his journal, which he later published under the title *The Cruise of the Portsmouth*. The following selection is from Joseph T. Downey's *Cruise of the Portsmouth* (n.d.).

Next morn [July 9, 1846] at daylight, a busy scene presented itself. All Hands were ordered to clean in "White Frocks, Blue Jackets & Trowsers, Black Hats and shoes" and the Call of All Hands to Muster even collected every soul on the Quarter Deck; when the Autocrat [John B. Montgomery, captain of the *Portsmouth*], all smiles and bows, read the Proclamation of the Commander in Chief, as also the General Order, and then proceeded to pick out the landing party, who were to guard the Flag to its destined place.

By 7 Bells matters were all arranged, and the party of Marines and Carbineers landed on the Bank, and after being marshalled in due order, the Band, consisting of one drum and one fife, struck up Yankee Doodle, and off we marched keeping time as best we might, to conquer the redoubtable town of Yerba Buena [San Francisco].

As we had anticipated, there was no foe to dispute our right of possession, for, save here and there a stray female face peeping from an Adobe wall, no living thing did we see, always excepting those invariable appendages to a Mexican Town, the Dogs, who looked on in mute astonishment and forgot in their wonder even to bark at us. On we went then in all the pride and pomp of Martial Array, over hill and dale, through sand and some little *mud*, until . . . we at last found ourselves brought up all standing in a hollow square, round the Flag Staff.

Here, had time allowed, our Old Man would no doubt have inflicted a speech if not a sermon upon us, but Fate decreed to the contrary, consequently the Flag was bent on to the Halyards and by a flourishing and patronising invitation, the whole of the male population of Yerba Buena, comprising, dogs and all, some 25 or 30 souls were called into the Square. The oration was delivered, the Proclamation read, and then the Autocrat with his own hands hoisted the Colors, while three hearty cheers from the bystanders, a prolonged howl from the dogs, and a salvo of 21 Guns from the Ship completed the Affair.

A party of Marines was now detached and ordered to occupy the Custom House as Barracks, and the remainder, with the Jacks, marched off for their boats in the same order they came up, the Band in the mean time making the air resound, for the first time in California, with the soul stirring melody of "Ole Dan Tucker," "It will never do to give it up so" and such like martial tunes. We now returned on board, and so for our part ended the first day of occupation of the town of Yerba Buena.

THE CONQUEST OF CALIFORNIA

Commodore Robert "Fighting Bob" Stockton, a younger officer, now replaced Commodore Sloat and soon completed the initial conquest of California—which was made almost entirely by the Navy. Frémont was commissioned a major and sent south in one ship to occupy San Diego, but Stockton himself sailed to San Pedro and then marched his sailors, unopposed, into Los Angeles. The *Californios* had no organized army, no help from Mexico, and at first little inclination to resist.

Lieutenant Archibald MacRae, USN, described this peaceful occupation of the California towns in an informal, chatty letter to his brother. The following selection is from Lieutenant MacRae's letter, October 25, 1846 (from George W. Smith and Charles Judah, eds., *Chronicles of the Gringos*).

The Naval Forces under Commodore Sloat landed in the face of a hot sun and took possession of Monterey and San Francisco, meeting with no other loss than that of two men who took the first opportunity of getting drunk, and quietly stowing themselves away in a pig sty, while the military force galloped up and down the country on horse back proclaiming every where that they were looking for Genl. Castro and his Army; this was done so that Castro might have no idea of their movements and therefore would not guard against a surprise.

The war having progressed so far the aged hero Commodore Sloat thinking that he had gained laurels enough gave up command of the squadron to Commodore Stockton and proceeded to the U. S. . . . Commodore Stockton . . . despatched the vessels down the coast and took possession of all the towns on the sea coast of upper California; besides which he arrested the French Consul at Monterey in consequence of his writing some very insolent letters protesting against our taking possession of the country; this may give us trouble.

No blood has been spilled on this side, nor have the hostile forces ever been near each other except in two instances, the first on the occasion spoken of [at Monterey] . . . and the last at the town of Angels (Pueblo de los Angeles). It was known from some very bombastic proclamations of Genl. Castro that he was at that place with nearly all his force—some five hundred men—in consequence of which the *Congress* proceeded to San Pedro (a small port 30 miles from the Pueblo) landed about 400 men and marched up. But unfortunately the General left a few hours before the Commodore arrived, and so no one had an opportunity of distinguishing himself. . . .

I have said that no blood has been spilled but here I am mistaken or rather had forgotten. Two troops of mounted men the command of which was given to two Pursers for God knows what reason, not being able to amuse themselves in any other way have been cooly [sic] shooting down some peaceful and friendly Indians. This occurred just before we left and therefore I do not know the full particulars, but all accounts agree upon the fact that deliberate murders have been committed upon a number of men who under the impression that they were to be put to death when ordered to arrange themselves in a line in front of the troop committed the very grave offence of attempting to escape, and who committed no other fault.

At present all Upper California (which extends from our Southern boundary to San Diego in Lat. 32° 40′ N) is in our possession, and the Mexican Coast is blockaded at all of its principal ports. . . .

It may appear singular to you that with so little force as we have employed out here the country could be taken possession of so quietly. But . . . the country is very thinly populated and the few Californians in it are divided . . . into three or four factions, so that any small number of resolute men—and such are those who are with Capt. Frémont—can do what they please. Besides this the number of Americans now in the territory is not much inferior to the number of Californians. . . . As for the towns on the coast, all put together would not be a match for one good frigate.

THE *CALIFORNIOS* REVOLT

Yankees and Spanish-speaking *Californios* were two contrasting peoples. The brown *Californios* were graceful and pleasure-loving. They were content with their somewhat run-down adobe ranch houses, their boundless acres, and herds of cattle and horses. They loved to ride, to dance, and to sing. They could sell enough cattle hides to make a little money—all they needed in their rural Arcadia.

The Yankee newcomers, on the other hand, looked at the land to see what cash crops they could raise. They were aggressive and progressive. They bought and sold from the *Californios* and made good profits. They did not want to wait until *mañana* (tomorrow) to complete a business deal. They wanted to "develop" the land—to find the best soil, establish fisheries, cut timber, prospect for minerals.

Californios in the past had been disgusted with the officials sent them from Mexico, disgusted with Mexican troops sometimes consisting chiefly of convicts. They had forced these officials and convicts out. But they remained loyal to their Spanish culture and Catholic religion. The Protestant Yankees, on the other hand, considered themselves a chosen people, destined to win the continent and bestow the blessings of democracy on the backward Spanish-speaking residents.

It is not surprising, therefore, that after the *Californios* accepted the first occupation of California, trouble should arise. Commodore Stockton had placed Captain Archibald Gillespie, a former secret agent, in charge of Los Angeles. But Gillespie introduced a strict martial law which angered the easygoing *Californios*. He forbade two of them to walk together in the streets, established a curfew, and banned amusements.

As a result, the *Californios* revolted. Under General José María Flores and other officers who had been paroled by Stockton, they besieged Gillespie and his fifty marines.

The following selection is from the proclamation signed by more than 300 indignant *Californios* (from Alfonso Trueba, *California: Tierra Perdida*).

> We, all the inhabitants of the Department of California, as members of the great Mexican nation, declare that our desire has been and is to stand, free and independent, under Mexico alone. The authorities established by the invader are illegitimate. We swear not to lay down our arms until the enemy has been expelled from our soil.

Every Mexican citizen from fifteen years of age to sixty who does not take up arms to carry out the plan will be declared a traitor under pain of death. Any Mexican or foreigner who directly or indirectly aids the enemy will suffer the same penalty. All property of every American resident who has directly or indirectly aided the enemy will be confiscated. Those who oppose this plan will be shot.

Gillespie and his garrison had to surrender but were allowed to depart to San Pedro. They promised to leave the area by ship.

At San Pedro, however, Gillespie met Yankee reinforcements—Captain William Mervine, who had just sailed down from the north. The "Paul Revere of California," one John Brown, had ridden 500 miles in five days to summon help. (The *Californios* called John Brown Juan Flaco—"Lean John.") So Gillespie forgot his promise and joined Mervine in an attempt to retake Los Angeles.

However, the Americans were defeated by Mexican General José Antonio Carrillo, in the "Battle of the Old Woman's Gun." A cannon, concealed by an old woman when the Yankees first occupied Los Angeles, turned the tide against the Americans. They had to sail back north, leaving San Diego besieged and the rest of southern California under Mexican rule.

THE BATTLE OF SAN PASCUAL

Meanwhile, in June, 1846, Washington had ordered the veteran General Stephen W. Kearny to lead 1,600 troops from Kansas to Santa Fe, New Mexico, and then on to California. Kearny's Army of the West was followed by 500 volunteers of the Mormon Battalion. The Mormons sang their song as they marched:

All hail the brave Battalion!
　　The noble, valiant band,
That went and served our country
　　With willing heart and hand.
Altho' we're called disloyal
　　By many a tongue and pen,
Our nation boasts no soldiers
　　So true as "Mormon" men.

Kearny took formal possession of New Mexico, with little or no opposition. Then, on September 25, 1846, he started for California. With him rode 300 dragoons in Union blue. But when Kearny met the famous scout Kit Carson and was told that California had already been conquered, he left 200 of these men in New Mexico. Carson, bearing dispatches from California, did not know about the recent revolt of the *Californios.*

Kearny insisted that Kit Carson guide him. He crossed the desert and mountains behind San Diego—and then ran into a hornets' nest. On a cold, rainy night his scouts reported red-mantled *Californio* lancers, encamped near the Indian village of San Pascual (close to present-day Escondido). These lancers, commanded by Andrés Pico, were hoping to ambush a foraging party of Americans from San Diego.

The clash that followed was the biggest battle actually fought on California soil. It was described by John M. Stanley, a draftsman on Kearny's staff. The following selection is from John M. Stanley's letter, January 19, 1847 (from George W. Smith and Charles Judah, eds., *Chronicles of the Gringos*).

　　From two Californians who were captured the hostile state of the country was ascertained; and the little band, without provisions save their horses, and almost destitute of water, pushed on their route.

On the morning of the 4th of December [1846] we resumed our march, Gen. Kearny having previously sent an express to San Diego to inform Commodore Stockton of his arrival in the country, and on the 5th we met Capt. Gillespie and Lieut. Beale, U. S. N., with an escort of thirty-five men.

After making a late camp, General Kearny heard that an armed body of Californians were encamped about nine miles from us. Lieut. Hammond, with a small party was sent out to reconnoitre. He returned about 12 o'clock, with the intelligence of a camp in the valley of San Pasqual, but learned nothing of the extent of the force, although it was thought to be about sixty.

The sentinel of the *Californios* heard dogs barking at midnight, and found a blanket marked "U. S." in the brush. Andrés Pico then quickly collected his horses from pasture and prepared for a fight.

At 2 o'clock on the morning of the 6th reveille sounded, and at 3 our force was formed in the order of battle and the march resumed. We arrived about daylight at the valley—the enemy were encamped about a mile from the declivity of the mountain over which we came, and . . . were waiting in their saddles for our approach.

From a misapprehension of an order, the charge was not made by our whole force, or with as much precision as was desirable; but the Californians retreated, on firing a single volley to an open plain about half a mile distant. Capt. Johnston and one private were killed in this charge. . . .

The retreat of the enemy was followed with spirit by our troops, skirmishing the distance of half a mile. When they reached the plains, our force was somewhat scattered in the pursuit. The Californians, taking advantage of this disorganization, fought with desperation, making great havoc with their lances, [crying *"Viva Mexico! Viva California!"*]. It was a real hand-to-hand fight, and lasted half an hour. They were, however, driven from the field, with what loss we could not learn.

We camped on the field and collected the dead. At first Gen. Kearny thought to move on the same day. The dead were lashed on mules, and remained two hours or more in that posture. It was a sad and melancholy picture.

We soon found, however, that our wounded were unable to travel. The mules were released of their packs, and the men engaged in fortifying the place for the night. During the day the enemy were in sight, curvetting their horses [making their horses prance], keeping our camp in constant excitement.

Three of Capt. Gillespie's volunteers started with despatches to Com. Stockton. The dead were buried at night, and ambulances made for the wounded; and the next morning we started, in face of the enemy's spies, being then about 38 miles from San Diego. In our march we were constantly expecting an attack. Spies could be seen upon the top of every hill. . . .

We had travelled about seven miles, when just before sunset we were attacked. The enemy came charging down a valley—about one hundred well mounted men. They were about dividing their force, probably with a view of attacking us in the front and rear, when Gen. Kearny ordered his men to take possession of a hill or hut on our left.

The enemy, seeing the movement, struck for the same point reaching it before us, and as we ascended they were pouring a very spirited fire upon us from behind the rocks. They were soon driven from the hill only one or two being wounded on our side. Here, therefore, we were compelled to encamp and also to destroy the more cumbersome of our camp equipage.

A white flag was sent by Señor Pico, the Californian commandant, and an exchange of prisoners effected—our bearers of despatches having been intercepted by the enemy.

We were more fortunate in getting an express through to San Diego for a reinforcement, and at the expiration of four days, during which we lived on the meat of mules, horses and colts, without bread or other condiment, we were joined by a reinforcement of two hundred men, and on the 11th of December resumed our march.

Not a Californian was to be seen as we proceeded, and on the 12th of December we reached San Diego, and received from the officers a hearty welcome.

THE HORSE MARINES

Fortunately for Kearny, "Fighting Bob" Stockton had arrived at San Diego in November, 1846. He had the men there to send to Kearny's rescue. Stockton had also collected horses and food supplies from Lower California. Now, with Kearny's assistance, he prepared to march north and retake Los Angeles.

March—or ride? Commodore Stockton decided to experiment with mounted marines. The following selection, describing the experiment, is from the irrepressible Joseph T. Downey's *Cruise of the Portsmouth* (n.d.).

A few days previous to the march [to Los Angeles], an idea popped into the brain of the Commodore [Stockton] that he would mount his Marines, thus forming a Corps of Horse Marines. . . . Accordingly, the Volunteers were ordered to bring their Horses, saddles, and other Equipment into the Square, and the Marines were ordered out and each man had an animal assigned him.

Now, as the Officer Commanding the Marines did not relish the plan at all, he paid but little attention to the distribution, and the volunteers cared not who got the Horses, since they were bound to lose them. In consequence the sharing out, was a one sided affair altogether. Long Marines got Short Horses, and Short Marines, Long Horses; those who were good Riders got gentle Horses and those who perhaps had never mounted a Horse, got the wildest of the Lot. . . . Well every man got his Horse at last, and having equipped himself with the enormous Spurs worn in this Country . . . grasped his musket, and awaited the word of command of mount.

The crowd was waiting with gaping mouths to see how the Horse Marines would work. "Mount" was the word and they did mount, and no sooner were they mounted, than a number were dismounted again. Then commenced a scene which soon convulsed the bystanders with Laughter, and convinced the Old Commander that his scheme would not work.

I have said a number were dismounted. I might have said a great number, but shall not, nor shall I say they were not at all particular how they dismounted . . . that some came over the head, and some over the stern of the Horses, some on the right, and more on the wrong side, nor how many legs were seen at once in the air, as their owners were describing involuntary sommersets, nor how muskets flew in all directions nor how some of the Horses ran away with their Riders and more without their Riders, how Marines, Muskets, caps and Horse Equippage was strewed . . . from one end of town to the other. Oh! no I shall say nothing about all this but I shall only say this scheme did not work.

THE WINDSTORM

On December 29, 1846, Stockton's blue jackets and Kearny's battered dragoons marched north to end the rebellion of the *Californios*. One of the more dangerous obstacles in their path, however, turned out to be "devil winds"—the dreaded California Santa Ana.

This east wind roars off the desert. Humidity drops almost to zero. The wind sears everything in its path; sand and dust lash the countryside. When it struck the Americans, they would have been helpless if *Californio* lancers had ridden them down from the windward.

The following selection, about the storm, is from Joseph T. Downey's *Cruise of the Portsmouth* (n.d.).

> Scarcely was the ground laid out and the camp formed when the wind breezed up, and steadily increasing, in the course of one half hour blew a perfect gale, and our Camp Ground, fore and aft, crosswise and cornerwise, was completely clouded and choked up with columns and moving masses of dust and fine sand. Look to windward you could not, for the least attempt at such a rash proceeding was sure to fill the Eyes, nose and mouth. . . . Men turned to one another to give orders and before the words were half uttered, they would be carried down your throat by a mass of dust. . . .
>
> The Camp was pitched however and here we had to lie. Tents were erected and fires lighted, but what was the use, a man might go and get his pot full of water, but before he could by any means coax it to

boil, it would be thickened to the consistency of mush by the cursed dust.

Bullocks were shot down, but no one would skin them . . . for 'twas of no avail, before you could have gotten the half of a Jacket off, the carcass would be smothered in sand and rendered unfit for eating.

To crown the whole, the Tents blew down, many of them with the occupants crowded in them, yet . . . they preferred remaining in them . . . to hazarding the attempt of facing that cloud of dust they knew to be their destiny outside. Growling, grumbling and cursing was the order of the day.

Many a poor fellow in pure desperation, would wind his blanket in many folds around his head, and cast himself upon the ground in mute despair and lay there until his body was nearly covered, but 'twas of no use, the fine dust and sand would penetrate even through the covering and he would rise, choaking and smothering, with eyes and nose full, and begin the world over again by a good cleaning out.

There was a deep trench or gully in this plain and here lots of men had taken up their sleeping places and found a sort of shelter here, but even there you were roused up every moment or two by some half blind and half smothered poor devil, who would stumble over you in the vain attempt to find a shelter for himself. . . .

The Commodore's [Stockton's] tent blew down among the rest, and he and his suite had to take a Cast for it, first having it securely propped up to Leeward to secure it from a Like mishap. There was one comfort however . . . and that was that there was no distinction of persons, no favors shown in this disbursement of dust. Officers and men all shared alike and every one dished an equal ration of Misery.

To mend the matter also, when at last the camp had become still, partly because no one wished to stir and partly because all those who might have wished to have done so were perfectly blinded, when those who had the least sign of shelter had got into a sort of drowse, Bang, Bang, went the Alarm Guns and to Arms, to Arms resounded through the camp.

All was hurry skurry, such a hunting for muskets and carbines, such feeling for pikes and pistols was never seen before. At last we got into some sort of a line, with our backs to the windward, for 'twas impossible to face it, and with shouldered arms awaited the attack, and had the Enemy known our situation and rode down upon us from the Windward they might have cut the whole command to pieces . . . easily . . . for when we were ordered to "right about face" every musket was down and every hand up to the eyes, digging for dear life for day light or at least for star-light and thus we were forced to stand.

CROSSING THE SAN GABRIEL

On January 7, 1847, the 600 troops of Stockton and Kearny arrived at the San Gabriel River. This is a small, muddy stream about three feet deep, south of Los Angeles. Here Mexican General José María Flores had fortified a hill on the Los Angeles side and was ready to make a stand.

The *Californios*, the best horsemen in the world, appeared on the crest of the hill. Their red capes and bright lances gleamed in the sunshine. The black mouths of cannon were visible against the winter-green slope. The Americans, Downey wrote, thought that soon some of them would "lie cold and motionless on the field of action . . . yet the knowledge did not . . . dissipate the good humor and hilarity which pervaded our Camp."

The following selection, describing the crossing of the San Gabriel, is from Joseph T. Downey's *Cruise of the Portsmouth* (n.d.).

At length we came to the Plain bordering the river [the San Gabriel], which is here about 2 miles wide, and runs on a gradual descent down to the River on one side, while on the other it rises to a small bank, then a plain some 2 or 3000 yards wide, and then rises another hill or embankment. The River of itself is some 30 or 40 yards in width and is in no place deeper than a man's hips but the bottom is formed of quicksand and is rather difficult to ford.

When we first came on to this plain, a halt was called and we took our dinner. . . . When the time of halt had elapsed we again formed in line of march and prepared to cross the river in face of the enemy. . . . Small parties [of *Californios*] could be seen from time to time, dodging and flying about among the hills . . . with their lances and sabres glittering in the sun.

The time for action had now arrived. We were formed in two columns marching by flank, while the Dragoons in front and the rear guard in the rear marching by company, formed a perfect square in the center of which were our Waggons, Carts, Cattle and Mules. . . . The Old General [Kearny] passed along the Line and as he passed gave words of advice and encouragement to Officers and Men. . . .

When we were about one half across the plain, the first shot on their part was fired. . . . They had planted their artillery on the second bank and directly in range of the fording place. . . . The first Shot however fell so far short of our ranks that it caused a laugh of derision from all in front . . . but as we were each moment drawing nearer . . . the Grape began to fly thick and fast and each moment may be our last.

The Dragoons have crossed the River headed by the Gallant Commodore, where are the artillery, why do they hesitate, why do they pause on the near bank of the River? An order has been given for them to unlimber and throw a few shot at the Enemy from this spot.

"Fighting Bob's" [Stockton's] dander is up, he dashes again into the River, recrosses and shouts at the top of his voice, "Not here, not here Limber up again, forward, we must, we will cross the River with these Guns."

Nothing can stay him, down into the River go the Mules, the Guns are heavy, the quicksand is hard to drag them through, the mules pause, one moment, and they are lost, off he comes from his horse, seizes the drag rope, "Now man, now pull for your lives, your commodore is here, dont desert him, dont for the love of God lose these guns," his words are fire to them, they seize hold, each man with a will, they move, they start and with a cheer over they go, while the water is ploughed in all directions by repeated discharges of grape, which flew like hail round them.

The Guns once crossed, the Commodore [Stockton] took charge of them himself. . . . In less than three discharges, a loud cheer from the Artillery men and Dragoons announced that he had capsized one of their Guns. . . .

While this was going on, the main body with the old Soldier [Kearny] at their head were steadily advancing; now they enter the water, the Old Fellow on his Mule, leading the way. . . . In the middle of the stream his mule stopped stock still, nor could he be persuaded to move another step; not at all disconcerted . . . the Old Soldier gathered his pistol in one hand, and with his riding whip in the other, he got off the Animal, and . . . kept on the same old pace and reached the bank at the head of the column.

The Americans took shelter behind a ridge just across the river, while the artillery dueled. Then the *Californios* prepared to charge.

> We were ordered to form to repel a charge of Cavalry. We rose to our feet and the sight was a Glorious one, down they came, in one long line, their Red Blankets, Black Hats and Bright Lances glittering in the sun. . . .
> Silently each front rank man drops upon his knee . . . then came the word "Fire" and . . . a sheet of fire flew along that line and the rattle of small arms added to the clangor of the day. . . . The cavalry paused in their mad career, and then turning . . . regained the cover of the Hill.
> Twice, thrice, did they attempt the same move . . . but twas all the same. . . . At length the proper moment arrived, and the Old Soldier, raising himself to the full height of his muscular frame, gave the word, "Now Jacks, at them, Charge, Charge and take the hill!"
> Like one man this mass arose from their hiding places and with a yell of fury dashed on to the Hill, with bayonets and Pikes at a charge . . . "Fighting Bob" and the "Old Soldier" side by side the one mad with excitement the other cool as a Julap.
> The foe paused but a moment, one look was

enough, they fled on all sides ... and when we gained the Hill there were no foemen there.

The Americans continued their march toward Los Angeles and on January 10, 1847, entered the city. According to William Emory, Kearny's chief of staff, "Flores, with 150 men ... fled to Sonora [Mexico], taking with him four or five hundred of the best horses and mules in the country. ... The silence of the Californians was now changed into deep and bitter curses upon Flores." The fighting in California was now at an end.

GRINGO RULE

The war between the United States and Mexico, like Rome's struggle with Carthage, had decisive results. The destiny of the North American continent—at least for two centuries—was determined when the United States took California and the Southwest from Mexico. This was half the territory of its southern neighbor. By the Treaty of Guadalupe Hidalgo (1848), Mexico lost its chance to become a great power.

The theory of American rule in California was set forth by General Kearny, who was appointed governor of the new territory. American constitutional guarantees of free speech, freedom of religion, free elections, and the protection of property were to be in force.

In practice, however, many Spanish-speaking citizens were cheated out of their property and otherwise discriminated against. A stunning discovery on the American River, near Sacramento, was to make the disorder even worse.

The following selection is from General Kearny's Proclamation to the People of California, March 1, 1847 (from John T. Hughes, *Doniphan's Expedition*).

The President of the United States having devolved on the undersigned the civil government of California, he enters upon the discharge of his duties with an ardent desire to promote . . . the interests of the country and well being of its inhabitants.

The undersigned is instructed by the President to respect and protect the religious institutions of California . . . since the constitution of the United States allows to every individual the privilege of worshipping his Creator, in whatever manner his conscience may dictate.

The undersigned is also instructed to protect the persons and property of peaceable inhabitants of the country, against each and every enemy, whether foreign or domestic. . . .

It is the desire and intention of the United States to procure for California as speedily as possible a free government like that of their own territories, and they will very soon invite the inhabitants to exercise the rights of free citizens in the choice of their own representatives, who may enact such laws as they deem best adapted to their interests and well being. But until this takes place, the laws actually in existence, which are not repugnant to the constitution of the United States, will continue in force. . . .

The undersigned . . . absolves all the inhabitants of California from any further allegiance to the republic of Mexico, and regards them as citizens of the United States. Those who remain quiet and peaceable will be protected in their rights. . . .

When Mexico involved the United States in war, the latter had not time to invite the Californians to join their standard as friends, but found themselves compelled to take possession of the country, to prevent its falling into the hands of some European power. In doing this, there is no doubt that some excesses, some unauthorized acts, were committed by persons in the service of the United States, and that in consequence, some of the inhabitants have sustained losses in their property. These losses shall be duly investigated, and those entitled to indemnification shall receive it.

For many years California has suffered great domestic convulsions; from civil wars, like poisoned fountains, have flowed calamity and pestilence over this beautiful region.—These fountains are now dried up; the stars and stripes now float over California . . . and under the protection of this flag agriculture must advance, and the arts and sciences will flourish like seed in a rich and fertile soil.

Americans and Californians! from henceforth one people. Let us then indulge one desire, one hope; let that be for the peace and tranquillity of our country. Let us unite like brothers, and mutually strive for the improvement and advancement of this our beautiful country. . . .

S. W. KEARNY, *Brig. Gen. U.S.A. and Governor of California*

6
"Gold! Gold! Gold from the American River!"

> Oh, California
>   That's the land for me.
> I'm bound for San Francisco
>   With my washbowl on my knee.
>   *Song of the Forty-Niners*

Sutter's Mill

EUREKA! GOLD IN THE MILLRACE

One Easterner who had migrated to California before the Mexican-American War was a "hard hat" mechanic from New Jersey, James Marshall. He had worked for Sutter and obtained a rancho for himself. During the war, he joined the California Battalion of Americans but returned to work with Sutter afterward.

The mechanic and the Swiss soldier of fortune Sutter became partners in a lumber business. To forward their business, Marshall journeyed up the American River and selected a spot, later called Coloma, for a sawmill.

Sutter gave Marshall some workmen, and the enterprising mechanic also hired some Indians, who had appeared and were watching curiously as the workmen felled trees. The sawmill was soon nearly finished, complete with a millrace—a channel or ditch—to provide waterpower to run the machines. James Marshall then had to leave for a few days but gave instructions for completing and widening this ditch.

The following selection tells what happened when Marshall returned and checked his millrace. It is from "James Marshall's Own Account of the Discovery of Gold in California" (from Valeska Bari, *The Course of Empire*).

> I returned in a few days and found everything favorable, all the men being at work in the ditch. When the channel was opened it was my custom every evening to raise the gate and let the water wash out as much sand and gravel through the night as possible;

and in the morning, while the men were getting breakfast, I would walk down, and shutting off the water, look along the race and see what was to be done....

One morning in January, it was a clear cold morning; I shall never forget that morning, as I was taking my usual walk along the race, after shutting off the water, my eye was caught by a glimpse of something shining in the bottom of the ditch. There was about a foot of water running there.

I reached my hand down and picked it up; it made my heart thump for I felt certain it was gold. The piece was about half the size and of the shape of a pea. Then I saw another piece in the water.

After taking it out, I sat down and began to think right hard. I thought it was gold, and yet it did not seem to be of the right color; all the gold coin I had seen was of a reddish tinge; this looked more like brass. I recalled to mind all the metals I had ever seen or heard of, but I could find none that resembled this.

Suddenly the idea flashed across my mind that it might be iron pyrites. I trembled to think of it! This question could soon be determined. Putting one of the pieces on hard river stone, I took another and commenced hammering it. It was soft and didn't break; it therefore must be gold, but largely mixed with some other metal, very likely silver; for pure gold, I thought, would certainly have a brighter color.

When I returned to our cabin for breakfast I showed the two pieces to my men. They were all a good deal excited, and had they not thought that the gold only existed in small quantities they would have abandoned everything and left me to finish the job alone. However, to satisfy them, I told them that as soon as we had the mill finished we would devote a week or two to gold hunting and see what we could make out of it.

While we were working in the race after this discovery, we always kept a sharp lookout, and in the course of three or four days we had picked up about three ounces—our work still progressing as lively as ever, for none of us imagined at that time that the whole country was sowed with gold.

About a week's time after the discovery I had to take another trip to the fort; and to gain what information I could respecting the real value of the metal, took all we had collected with me and showed it to Mr. Sutter, who at once declared it was gold, but thought with me, it was greatly mixed with some other metal.

It puzzled us a great deal to hit upon the means of telling the exact quantity contained in the alloy; however, we at last stumbled on an old American cyclopedia where we saw the specific gravity of all the metals, and rules given to find the quantity of each in a given bulk. After hunting over the whole fort and borrowing from some of the men, we got three dollars and a half in silver, and with a small pair of scales we soon cyphered it out that there was no silver nor copper in the gold, but that it was entirely pure.

This fact being ascertained, we thought it our best policy to keep it as quiet as possible till we should have finished our mill, but there was a great number of disbanded Mormon soldiers in and about the fort, and when they came to hear of it, why, it just spread like wildfire, and soon the whole country was in a bustle. I had scarcely arrived at the mill again till several persons appeared with pans, shovels and hoes, and those that had not iron picks had wooden ones, all anxious to fall to work and dig up our mill; but this we would not permit.

As fast as one party disappeared another would arrive, and sometimes I had the greatest kind of trouble to get rid of them. I sent them all off in different directions, telling them about such and such places, where I was certain there was plenty of gold if they would only take the trouble of looking for it.

At that time I never imagined the gold was so abundant. I told them to go to such and such places, because it appeared that they would dig nowhere but in such places as I pointed out, and I believe such was their confidence in me that they would have dug on the very top of yon mountain if I had told them to do so.

So there, stranger, is the entire history of the gold discovery in California—a discovery that hasn't as yet been of much benefit to me.

Gold had actually been discovered before in California. Mission Indians had carried yellow nuggets to the Franciscans, who warned them not to tell anyone about the metal—otherwise, greedy strangers would come and seize the Indians' lands. (The Franciscans were good prophets.) A Spaniard discovered a small cache of gold in 1841; another cache was found in 1842, in southern California. But the San Feliciano Canyon lode of 1842 received only local publicity and was soon worked out.

Marshall's find, on the other hand, was publicized by the Mormon merchant Sam Brannan, who rode down the main street of San Francisco swinging his hat in his hand and shouting, "Gold! Gold! Gold from the American River!"

For James Marshall, as for Sutter, the discovery of gold was a disaster. Marshall himself never found any pay dirt. Mobs surrounded him wherever he went, threatening him unless he would guide them to a rich lode. Squatters occupied and ruined his ranch, and he died a poor man.

SPREADING THE NEWS

When gold was discovered, January 24, 1848, the total non-Indian population of California was around 20,000. Just ten months later, the Yankee alcalde (mayor) of Monterey, the Reverend Walter Colton, wrote in his diary: "Some fifty thousand persons are drifting up and down these slopes of the great Sierra [Nevada], of every hue, language, and clime. . . . All are in quest of gold."

Faster than the shot fired at Concord, the news of Marshall's find was heard around the world. Horace Greeley ran a two-column "Golden Chronicle" every day about California discoveries, on the front page of his New York *Tribune*. President Polk informed Congress about the unbelievable "abundance of gold," verified by "the authentic reports of officers in the public service." Soon the peace-loving Mexican alcalde of San Jose, Captain Juan Fernández, could write:

"Australia sent criminals, Italy musicians, Germany barbers and beer drinkers, England pugilists, France bullies and prostitutes, Mexico monte players [gamblers], Chile sneak thieves and pickpockets, Peru malefactors, Ireland highway robbers, and the United States politicians and plotters and also, now and then, a man of property with his following of artisans and farmers."

The forty-niners from the States came by three routes. By ship around Cape Horn took from six to nine months. By sea to Panama, across the Isthmus, and then by sea to San Francisco might require three months or three years—because it was hard to obtain a passage up the Pacific. By land, in prairie schooners across the continent, was four months, with luck. In 1849, 30,000 emigrants took the prairie route.

"The poor women arrive, looking as haggard as so many Endorean witches," wrote one observer near Sacramento. "Burnt to the color of a hazel-nut, with their hair cut short, and its gloss entirely destroyed by the alkali. . . . You will hardly find a family that has not left some beloved one buried upon the plains."

In the selection below, the Reverend Walter Colton describes the outbreak of "gold fever" in Monterey. Colton, a Navy chaplain, had been appointed alcalde of Monterey in 1846, when American naval forces occupied the town. He was a Vermonter of delicate health—in spite of his ruddy complexion—but with strong literary interests. The selection is from his *Three Years in California,* first published in 1850.

TUESDAY, JUNE 20.

My messenger sent to the mines, has returned with specimens of the gold; he dismounted in a sea of upturned faces. As he drew forth the yellow lumps from his pockets, and passed them around among the eager crowd, the doubts, which had lingered till now, fled. All admitted they were gold, except one old man, who still persisted they were some Yankee invention, got up to reconcile the people to the change of flag.

The excitement produced was intense; and many were soon busy in their hasty preparations for a departure to the mines. The family who had kept house for me caught the moving infection. Husband and wife were both packing up; the blacksmith dropped his hammer, the carpenter his plane, the mason his trowel, the farmer his sickle, the baker his loaf, and the tapster his bottle. All were off for the mines, some on horses, some on carts, and some on crutches, and one went in a litter.

An American woman, who had recently established a boardinghouse here, pulled up stakes, and was off before her lodgers had even time to pay their bills. Debtors ran, of course. I have only a community of women left, and a gang of prisoners, with here and there a soldier, who will give his captain the slip at the first chance....

TUESDAY, JULY 18.

Another bag of gold from the mines, and another spasm in the community. It was brought down by a sailor from Yuba river, and contains a hundred and thirty-six ounces. It is the most beautiful gold that has appeared in the market; it looks like the yellow scales of the dolphin, passing through his rainbow hues at death.

My carpenters, at work on the school-house, on seeing it, threw down their saws and planes, shouldered their picks, and are off for the Yuba. Three seamen ran from the *Warren*, forfeiting their four years' pay; and a whole platoon of soldiers from the fort left only their colors behind....

IN THE DIGGINGS

Soon the mountains of northern California were swarming with free-lance prospectors. The prospector wore "a flannel shirt,—almost always of a dark blue color—pantaloons with the boots drawn up over them, and a low-crowned, broad-brimmed, black felt hat." His tools were pick and shovel and pan, all "worth their weight in gold" because of the demand for equipment.

How did he prospect for gold? What luck did the average miner have? A Philadelphia schoolteacher, Daniel

Woods, has given a good picture of the trials of the anonymous forty-niner.

Woods walked out of his classroom in 1849 and sailed with a company of Americans to Tampico, Mexico. Here, in the warm tropics, he donned gloves and slept "in a bag made of cotton" pulled up over his head, to avoid being devoured by mosquitoes. He and his companions dodged guerrillas on their rugged ride across Mexico, then took passage on a ship that carried them up the west coast to San Francisco.

Some of their experiences in the "diggings" are narrated in the following selection. It is from Daniel Woods' "Across Mexico and Life in the Diggings" (from Valeska Bari, *The Course of Empire*).

Salmon Falls, South Fork of the American River—July 4.

Here we are, at length, in the gold diggings. Seated around us, upon the ground, beneath a large oak, are a group of wild Indians, from the tribe called "Diggers." They have brought us in some salmon, one of which weighs 29 pounds. These they spear with great dexterity, and exchange for provisions, or clothing, and ornaments of bright colors.

We are surrounded on all sides by high, steep mountains, over which are scattered the evergreen and white oak, and which are inhabited by the wolf and bear. We have spent the day in "prospecting," a term which designates a very important part of the business of mining. In order to find the gold the ground must be prospected.

A spot is first selected, in the choice of which science has little and chance everything to do. The stones and loose upper soil, as also the subsoil, almost down to the primitive rock, are removed. Upon or near this rock most of the gold is found, and it is the object in every mining operation, to reach this rock, however great the labor, even though it lies forty, eighty or one hundred feet beneath the surface.

If, when this strata rock is attained, it is found to present a smooth surface, it may as well be abandoned at once; if seamed with crevices, running at angles with the river, the prospect of the miner is favorable. Some of the dirt is then put into a pan, taken to the water and washed out with great care. The miner stoops down by the stream and dipping a quantity of water into the pan with the dirt, stirs it about with his hands, washing and throwing out the large pebbles, till the dirt is thoroughly wet.

More water is then taken into the pan, the whole mass well stirred and shaken, and the top gravel thrown off with the fingers while the gold, being heavier, sinks deeper into the pan. It is then shaken about, more water being continually added, and thrown off with a sideway motion which carries with it the dirt at the top, while the gold settles yet lower down. When the dirt is nearly washed out great care is requisite to prevent the lighter scales of gold from being washed out with the sand.

At length a ridge of gold scales, mixed with a little sand, remains in the pan, from the quantity of which some estimate may be formed of the richness of the place. If there are five to eight grains it is considered that it will pay. If less, the miner digs deeper or opens a new hole, until he finds a place affording a good prospect. When this is done he sets his cradle by the side of the stream and proceeds to wash all the dirt.

Thus have we been employed the whole of this day, digging one hole after another, washing out many test pans, hoping at every new attempt to find that which would reward our toil—and we have made ten cents each.

July 7th.

This morning witnessed an instance of that remarkable success in mining which rarely occurs but which, when it does occur, turns the heads of so many. I might aptly quote Virgil's figurative description of Rumor and apply it to these gold stories. They go out quite respectable in appearance, furnished with hat and cane at the start, but as they proceed they suddenly expand to the proportions of Hercules, with his trunk of a tree for a club. We met this story long afterward after it had returned from its voyage to the States and to Europe, and but for its having claimed Salmon Falls as its birthplace it could not have been recognized at all.

The facts were these: Two Irishmen followed the lead of the Jordan Brothers who, in a few weeks, made $3,000 and are now on their way home. They commenced at the edge of the bar and were so lucky as to find the vein which the Jordans had found. This vein is about seven inches wide, ten feet below the surface of the bank, and is imbedded in a stratum of hard clay. Before breakfast this morning these two Irishmen, who never before owned a savings in their lives, took out $422.

We were working within three yards of them and I have been compelled to contrast our own small operations with their brilliant success.

July 9th.

Today we made $20 each. One of the conclusions at which we are rapidly arriving is that the chances of our making a fortune in the gold mines are about the same as those in favor of our drawing a prize in a lottery. No kind of work is so uncertain. A miner may happen upon a good location in his very first attempt and in a very few days make hundreds or thousands, while the experienced miners about him may do nothing.

An instance of this kind happened recently when two men who had been some time in the mines started a dispute as to a small space between their claims. As they could not amicably settle the dispute they agreed to leave it to a newcomer who happened by who had not yet done an hour's work in the mines. He measured off ten feet—the amount allowed by custom—to each of the claimants, taking for his trouble the narrow strip of land between them. In a few hours the larger claims belonging to the older miners were abandoned as useless while the newcomer discovered a deposit which yielded him $7,435.

July 10th.

We made $3.00 each today. This life of hardships and exposure has affected my health. Our diet consists of hard tack, flour we eat half cooked, and salt pork, with occasionally a salmon which we purchase from the Indians. Vegetables are not to be procured.

Our feet are wet all day, while a hot sun shines down upon our heads and the very air parches the skin like the hot air of an oven. Our drinking water comes to us thoroughly impregnated with the mineral substances washed through the thousand cradles above us.

After our days of labor, exhausted and faint, we retire—if this word may be applied to the simple act of lying down in our clothes—robbing our feet of their boots to make a pillow of them, and wrapping our blankets about us, on a bed of pine boughs, or on

The Forty-niners

Stamping machine, used to crush gold ore

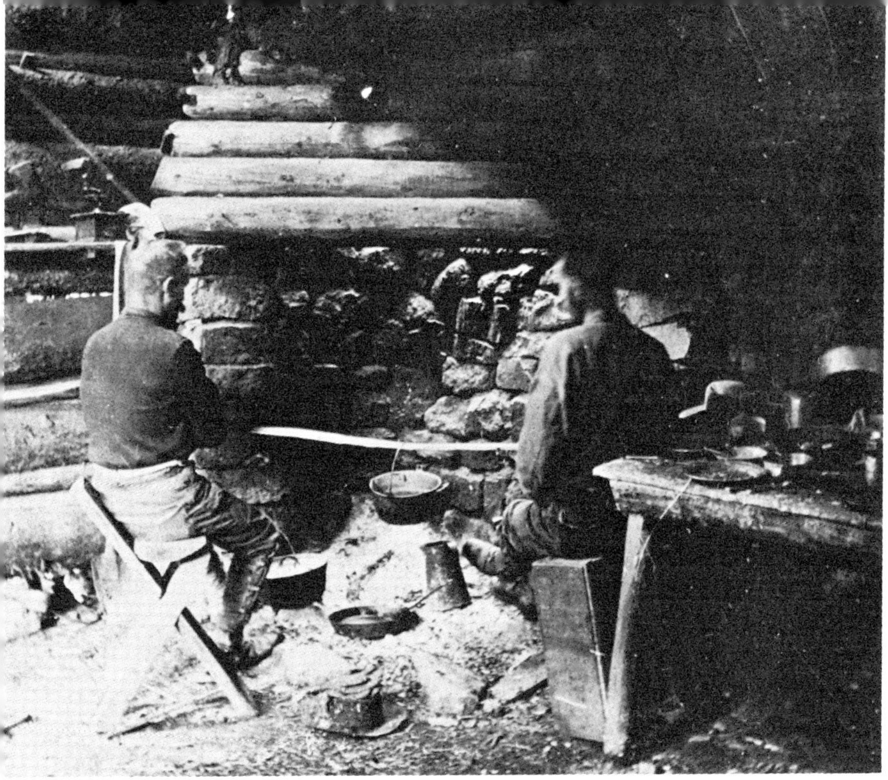

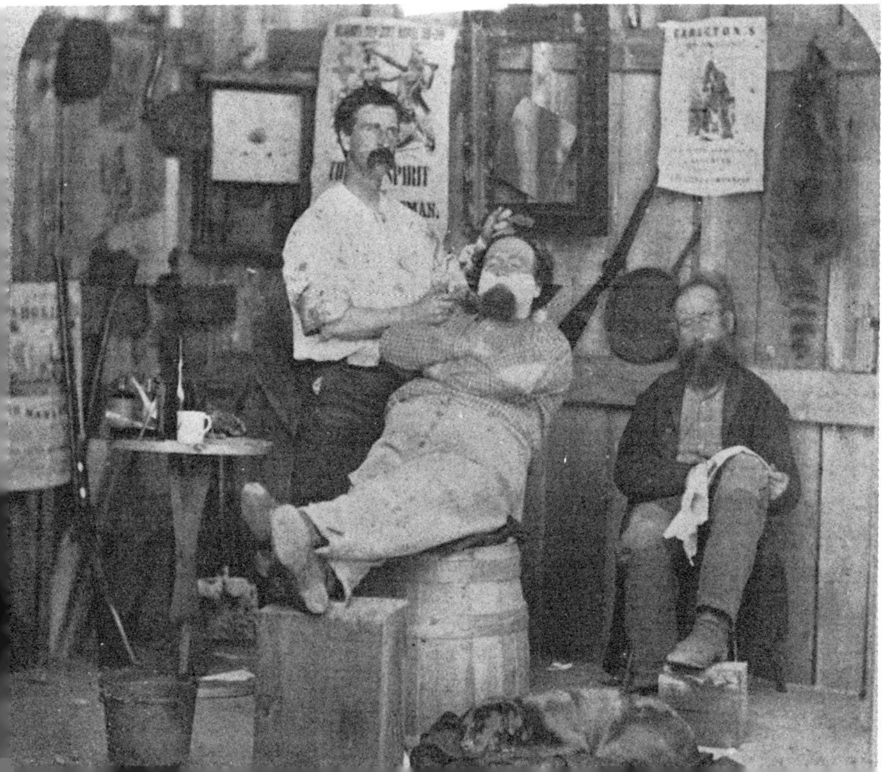

the ground beneath the clear, bright stars of the night. Near morning there is always a change in the temperature and several blankets become necessary.

The feet and the hands of a novice in this business become blistered and lame, and the limbs are stiff. Besides all these causes of sickness, the anxieties and cares which wear away the lives of so many men who leave their families to come to this land of gold, contribute, in no small degree, to the same result.

BOOM TOWN

One of the biggest problems of the miners was obtaining their grubstake—their supplies. They needed towns in the wilderness, to serve as bases.

So towns sprang up overnight. A waffle pattern of streets and lots would be stamped on a clearing by a river. Then came the merchants with their blankets ($40 apiece), boots ($100 a pair), eggs ($3 each), butter ($6 a pound), medicines ($10 a pill), and so on. Speculators made fortunes in real estate. Gamblers set up houses for the influx of miners in the winter, when snow blocked the Sierra trails.

An important town born of this population explosion was Marysville. Marysville lay north of Sacramento, near the junction of the Feather and Yuba rivers, close to many mining claims.

A thirty-three-year-old lawyer who was considered an "old man" by the generally youthful prospectors played an important part in its founding. Stephen Field, the lawyer, was a brother of the Cyrus Field who laid the first Atlantic cable. He was competent and energetic, arriving from New York filled with the buoyant optimism of most newcomers.

In the selection below, Field tells how the "instant city"

of Marysville was organized, complete with laws and an elected mayor, in just a few days. The selection is from Stephen Field's "Justice in '49" (from Valeska Bari, *The Course of Empire*).

Among the letters of introduction which I had brought was one to the firm of Simmons, Hutchinson & Company, who received me cordially and inquired particularly of my intentions as to residence and business. They stated that there was a town at the head of navigation, at the juncture of the Sacramento and Feather rivers which offered inducements to a young lawyer. They called it "Vernon" and said they owned some lots which they would sell to me.

I replied that I had no money. That made no difference, they said, I could have them on credit, they desired to build up the town. . . . The steamer *McKim* was going next day to Sacramento and they offered me a ticket, which I took.

It was the time of the great flood of that year and upon reaching Sacramento, we took a small boat and rowed up to the hotel. There I found a great crowd of enthusiastic people, all talking about California and all in the highest spirits. . . .

The next day I took the steamer *Lawrence* for Vernon. The boat was so heavily laden as to be only eighteen inches out of water and the passengers were requested not to move about the deck but to remain as quiet as possible. Three or four hours after leaving Sacramento, the captain suddenly cried out with great energy: "Stop her! Stop her!" and with some difficulty the boat escaped running into what seemed to be a solitary house standing in a vast lake of water.

I asked what place that was, and was answered: "Vernon,"—the town where I had been advised to settle as affording a good opening for a young lawyer.

I turned to the captain and said I had decided to go on further.

Two days later we arrived at a place called "Nye's Ranch," near the junction of the Feather and Yuba Rivers. No sooner had the vessel touched the landing than all the passengers, as though moved by a common impulse, started for an old adobe building, near which were numerous tents. By the number of tents there must have been five hundred or a thousand people there. In the main room of the adobe was a map spread out on the counter, containing the plan of a town. Behind stood a man crying out:

"Gentlemen, put your names down; put your names down, all that want lots."

I asked the price of lots.

"Two hundred and fifty dollars each for lots 80x160 feet."

"But suppose a man puts his name down and afterwards doesn't want the lots?"

"You need not take them if you don't want them. Put your names down, gentlemen, put your names down."

I took him at his word and put my name down for sixty-five lots, aggregating $16,250.00. This produced a great sensation. I had at the time not more than twenty dollars, but it was immediately noised about that a great capitalist had arrived from San Francisco to invest in lots in this rising town. The proprietor of the place waited upon me and showed me great attention. . . .

I saw at once that the place, from its position at the head of practical navigation, was destined to become an important depot for the neighboring mines and that its beauty and salubrity would make it a pleasant place for residence.

Upon inquiry I found that the proprietors had purchased the land and several leagues of land adjoining from Captain John A. Sutter, but had not yet received a conveyance of the property. I offered to draw the deed and they sent for Captain Sutter to sign it, but when the deed was signed there was no officer to take the acknowledgment nor an office in which it could be recorded, nearer than Sacramento.

I suggested that . . . there should be an office to record deeds and a magistrate to preserve order. A new house, the frame of which had been brought up by the steamer, had been put up that day, and a gentleman suggested that we meet there that evening to celebrate the signing of the deed and to consider organizing the town.

When evening came, the house was filled. Two baskets of champagne added cheer to the occasion. I was called on to make a speech, which I did in most glowing colors. A public meeting was arranged for the following morning for the organization of government.

The following afternoon election of officers took place. My nomination as *alcalde* followed but I was not to have office without a struggle. An opposition candidate appeared and an exciting election ensued. The main objection urged against me was that I was a newcomer. I had been there only three days, my opponent had been there six. I beat him, however, by nine votes. . . .

Soon after election I went to San Francisco to get my belongings and while there purchased, on credit, a frame house and several zinc houses which were at once shipped to Marysville [the new town]. I opened my office in the frame house and exercised not only the functions of magistrate and justice but also of a supervisor of the town. I opened books for the recording of deeds and conveyances. I appointed an active and courageous person to act as marshal and peace and order were preserved, not only in Marysville but for miles around....

As to my speculations, in a short time after writing my name down for sixty-five lots in Marysville, property increased tenfold in value. Within ninety days I sold $25,000.00 worth and still had most of my lots left. My frame and zinc houses rented for $1000.00 a month. The emoluments of my office as *alcalde* were large. In criminal cases I received no fee for my services and in civil cases the fees were small, but in the recording of deeds the fees amounted to a large sum.

At one time I had $14,000.00 in gold dust in my safe. It is only fair to add, however, that the following year, I engaged in other speculations in which I lost all that I had made more quickly than I had acquired it and found myself also in debt.

A MINER'S CABIN

One day, in the summer of 1851, a young woman—"a shivering, frail, homeloving little thistle," as she described herself—rode her "darling little mule" down a wild California canyon. With her doctor husband, Louise Clappe entered the tiny mining community of Rich Bar. It perched on a bank of the North Fork of the Feather River, above Marysville.

In her writings, Louise called herself "Dame Shirley." She and her husband had arrived in San Francisco in 1849, and she had marveled at the city's "flashy looking squares, built one day and burnt the next." But the fogs and cold winds sweeping through the Golden Gate hurt the doctor's health. Early in 1851, he had established himself in Rich Bar, in invigorating mountain country. Now he was bringing "Dame Shirley" to join him.

At the sight of his "office"—a nondescript cabin with dirt floor and a few benches for the patients to sit on—she burst out laughing. Orphaned in New Jersey and reared in western Massachusetts, "Dame Shirley" had the vitality of youth, of all the young "Argonauts" (gold-seekers) who were exuberantly taking over the land.

She and the doctor would stay in Rich Bar, and adjoining Indian Bar, for little more than a year. During that time, she would write twenty-three letters to her sister Molly, back in Massachusetts. In them, she would give what one historian has said is "the best account of an early mining camp that is known to me." Bret Harte would base several of his most famous short stories on these letters.

"I take pains," "Dame Shirley" wrote her sister, "to describe things exactly as I see them, hoping that thus you will obtain an idea of life in the mines *as it is.*"

The following selection, a description of the cabin which "Dame Shirley" and Dr. Clappe later moved into, is "perhaps the best we have of an early habitation in one of the more remote diggings." It is from Louise Clappe's *The Shirley Letters*, first published 1854–55.

From our Log Cabin, Indian Bar,
October 7, 1851 . . .

The bar is so small, that it seems impossible that the tents and cabins scattered over it can amount to a dozen; there are, however, twenty in all, including those formed of calico shirts and pine boughs. With the exception of the paths leading to the different tenements, the entire level is covered with mining holes, on the edges of which lie the immense piles of dirt and stones which have been removed from the excavations.

There is a deep pit in front of our cabin and another at the side of it; though they are not worked, as when "prospected," they did not "yield the color."

Not a spot of verdure is to be seen on this place; but the glorious hills rising on every side vested in foliage of living green, make ample amends for the sterility of the tiny level upon which we camp. . . .

The river [Río de las Plumas] in hue of a vivid emerald—as if it reflected the hue of the fir trees above,—bordered with a band of dark red, caused by the streams flowing into it from the different sluices, ditches, long-toms, etc., which meander from the hill just back of the Bar, wanders musically along.

Across the river and in front of us, rises nearly perpendicularly, a group of mountains, the summits of which are broken into many beautifully cut conical and pyramidal peaks. At the foot and left of these eminences, and a little below our Bar, lies Missouri Bar, which is reached from this spot by a log bridge. Around the latter, the river curves in the shape of a crescent. . . .

At present the sun does not condescend to shine upon Indian Bar at all, and the old settlers tell me that he will not smile upon us for the next three months; but he nestles lovingly in patches of golden glory, all along the brows of the different hills around us. . . .

The first artificial elegance which attracts your vision, is a large rag shanty, roofed, however, with a rude kind of shingles, over the entrance of which is painted in red capitals . . . the name of the great Humboldt spelt without the *d*. This is the only hotel in this vicinity, and as there is a really excellent bowling alley attached to it, and the bar-room has a floor upon which the miners can dance, and, above all, a cook who can play the violin, it is very popular.

But the clinking of glasses, and the swaggering air of some of the drinkers, reminds us that it is no place for a lady, so we will pass through the dining room and emerging at the kitchen, in a step or two reach our log cabin.

Enter, my dear; you are perfectly welcome; besides, we could not keep you out if we would, as there is not even a latch on the canvas door, though we really intend in a day or two to have a hook put on to it.

The room into which we have just entered is about twenty feet square. It is lined over the top with white cotton cloth, the breadths of which being sewed together only in spots, stretch gracefully apart in many places, giving one a birds-eye view of the shingles above. The sides are hung with a gaudy chintz, which I consider a perfect marvel of calico printing. . . .

A curtain of the above described chintz . . . divides off a portion of the room, behind which stands a bedstead. . . .

The fireplace is built of stones and mud, the chimney finished off with alternate layers of rough sticks and this same rude mortar; contrary to the usual custom, it is built inside, as it was thought that arrangement would make the room more comfortable; and you may imagine the queer appearance of this unfinished pile of stones, mud and sticks. The mantlepiece . . . is formed of a beam of wood, covered with strips of tin procured from cans, upon which still remain in black hieroglyphics, the names of the different eatables they formerly contained. Two smooth stones . . . do duty as fire-dogs.

I suppose that it would be no more than civil to call a hole two feet square in one side of the room, a window, although it is as yet guiltless of glass. . . . F. has sent to Marysville for some glass, though it is the general opinion that the snow will render the trail impassable for mules before we can get it. In this case, we shall tack up a piece of cotton cloth, and should it chance at any time to be very cold, hang a blanket before the opening. . . .

My toilet table is formed of a trunk elevated upon two claret cases, and by draping it with some more of the blue linen neatly fringed, it really will look quite handsome. . . . The looking-glass is one of those which come in paper cases for doll's houses. . . . The washstand is another trunk covered with a towel, upon which you will see for bowl, a large vegetable dish, for ewer, a common sized dining pitcher; near this, upon a small cask, is placed a pail, which is daily filled with water from the river. . . .

We have four chairs. . . . An ingenious individual in the neighborhood . . . made me a sort of wide bench, which covered with a neat plaid, looks quite sofa-like. A little pine table with oil-cloth tacked over the top of it, stands in one corner of the room, upon which are arranged the chess and cribbage boards. There is a larger one for dining purposes. . . . I must mention that the floor is so uneven that no article of furniture gifted with four legs pretends to stand upon but three at once, so that the chairs, tables, etc., remind you constantly of a dog with a sore foot.

At each end of the mantle-piece is arranged a candle-stick, not, much to my regret, a block of wood with a hole in the centre of it, but a real brittania-ware candle-stick; the space between is gaily ornamented with F.'s meerschaum, several styles of clay pipes, cigars, cigaritos, and every procurable variety of tobacco. . . . In lieu of a bookcase . . . [there] is . . . a candle-box, which contains the library, consisting of a bible and prayer-book, Shakespeare, Spenser, Coleridge, Shelley, Keats, Lowell's Fable for Critics, Walton's Complete Angler [sic] and some Spanish books. . . .

There, my dainty Lady Molly, I have given you . . . a . . . minute description of my new home. How would you like to winter in such an abode? in a place where there are no newspapers, no churches, lectures, concerts or theaters; no fresh books, no shopping, calling nor gossiping little tea-drinkings; no parties, no balls, no picnics, no *tableaux*, no charades, no latest fashions, no daily mail, (we have an express once a month,) no promenades, no rides nor drives; no vegetables but potatoes and onions, no milk, no eggs, no *nothing*?

A FUNERAL

Not long after "Dame Shirley" came to Rich Bar, there was a funeral. Nancy Ann Bailey, twenty-six years old, died of peritonitis, leaving an infant and a little girl without a mother.

"Dame Shirley" described the funeral with a simple realism that is perhaps more moving than the pathos of Bret Harte's famous depiction of the dead mother in "The Luck of Roaring Camp."

The following selection is from Louise Clappe's *The Shirley Letters*, first published 1854–55.

Rich Bar, East Branch of the
North Fork of Feather River,
September 22, 1851

It seems indeed awful, dear M., to be compelled to announce to you the death of one of the four women forming the female population of this Bar. I have just returned from the funeral of poor Mrs. B., who died of peritonitis, (a common disease in this place) after an illness of four days only....

Her funeral took place at ten this morning. The family reside in a log-cabin at the head of the Bar.... Everything in the room, though of the humblest description, was exceedingly clean and neat.

On a board, supported by two butter-tubs, was extended the body of the dead woman, covered with a sheet; by its side stood the coffin of unstained pine, lined with white cambric....

The bereaved husband held in his arms a sickly babe ten months old, which was moaning piteously for its mother. The other child, a handsome, bold-looking little girl six years of age, was running gaily around the room perfectly unconscious of her great bereavement. A sickening horror came over me, to see her every few moments, run up to her dead mother, and peep laughingly under the hankerchief, that covered her moveless face.

Poor little thing! It was evident that her baby-toilet had been made by men; she had on a new calico dress, which, having no tucks in it, trailed to the floor, and gave her a most singular and dwarf-womanly appearance.

About twenty men, with the three women of the place, had assembled at the funeral. An *extempore* prayer was made, filled with all the peculiarities usual to that style of petition. Ah! how different from the soothing verses of the glorious burial service of the church.

As the procession started for the hill-side graveyard—a dark cloth cover, borrowed from a neighboring monte-table, was flung over the coffin. Do not think that I mention any of these circumstances in a spirit of mockery; far from it. Every observance, usual on such occasions, that was *procurable,* surrounded this funeral. All the gold on Rich Bar could do no more; and should I die to-morrow, I should be marshaled to my mountain grave beneath the same monte-table cover pall, which shrouded the coffin of poor Mrs. B.

I almost forgot to tell you, how painfully the feelings of the assembly were shocked by the sound of the nails—there being no screws at any of the shops—driven with a hammer into the coffin, while closing it. It seemed as if it *must* disturb the pale sleeper within.

WILDERNESS SOUNDS

Many centuries ago, a Christian saint, St. Jerome, went to the desert to seek peace but found the barren waste overrun with quarreling monks. Likewise, "Dame Shirley," who loved the quiet beauty of nature, now heard a few discordant notes under her "blue California Heaven."

The following selection is from Louise Clappe's *The Shirley Letters,* first published 1854–55.

> *Rich Bar, East Branch of the*
> *North Fork of Feather River,*
> *September 30, 1851*

I think that I have never spoken to you of the mournful extent to which profanity prevails in California. . . . Of course the most vulgar blackguard will abstain from swearing in the *presence* of a lady; but in this rag and card-board house [the Empire Hotel], one is *compelled* to hear the most sacred of names constantly profaned by the drinkers and gamblers. . . .

Some of these expressions, were they not so fearfully blasphemous, would be grotesquely sublime. For instance; not five minutes ago, I heard two men quarrelling in the street, and one said to the other, "only let me get hold of your beggarly carcase [sic] once, and I will use you up so small that God Almighty himself cannot see your *ghost!*" . . .

But it is not the swearing alone which disturbs my slumber. There is a dreadful flume, the machinery of which, keeps up the most dismal moaning and shrieking all the livelong night—painfully suggestive of a suffering child. . . . A flume . . . in an immense trough, which takes up a portion of the river, and, with the aid of a dam, compels it to run in another channel, leaving the vacated bed of the stream ready for mining purposes. . . .

But to return to my sleep murderers. The rolling on the bowling alley never leaves off for ten consecutive minutes at any time during the entire twenty-four hours. It is a favorite amusement at the mines; and the only difference that Sunday makes, is, that then it never leaves off for *one* minute.

Besides the flume and the bowling alley, there is an inconsiderate dog, which *will* bark from starry even till dewy morn. I fancy that he has a wager on the subject, as all the other *puppies* seem bitten by the betting mania.

LONG TOMS AND COYOTE HOLES

By "surface scraping and gouging . . . the frantic work of amateurs," $4,000,000 in gold was collected in 1848. The "island named California" did indeed possess streams whose banks were sprinkled with the yellow grains, just as romance writer Ordóñez de Montalvo had imagined it.

The gold was originally veined in rocks. Owing to weathering and disintegration of the rocks, under the action of water, it was washed down mountain streams. There its weight caused it to sink to the gravel at the bottom. In bedrock near the streams, other rich veins were found. Eventually, from the mother lode, more than $1 billion would be extracted.

One day "Dame Shirley" decided to try to describe the methods used in this frantic scramble for gold. Before explaining the system and machines, she apologized for this "dreadfully commonplace and severely utilitarian" letter. But her account is now considered "the most satisfying and clearly expressed brief discussion of actual mining customs and methods in the heyday of the California diggings."

The following selection, from this letter, is from Louise Clappe's *The Shirley Letters,* first published 1854–55.

From our Log Cabin, Indian Bar, April 10, 1852 . . .

First, let me explain to you the "claiming" system. As there are no State laws upon the subject, each mining community is permitted to make its own. Here, they have decided that no man may "claim" an area of more than forty feet square. This he "stakes off" and puts a notice upon it, to the effect that he "holds" it for mining purposes. If he does not choose to "work it" immediately, he is obliged to renew the notice every ten days; for without this precaution, any other person has a right to "jump it," that is, to take it from him.

There are many ways of evading the above law. For instance, an individual can "hold" as many "claims" as he pleases, if he keeps a man at work in each, for this workman represents the original owner. I am told, however, that the laborer, himself, can "jump" the "claim" of the very man who employs him, if he pleases so to do. This is seldom, if ever, done; the person who is willing to be hired, generally prefers to receive the six dollars *per diem,* of which he is *sure* in any case, to running the risk of a "claim" not proving valuable....

Having got our gold mines discovered, and "claimed," I will try to give you a faint idea of how they "work" them. Here, in the mountains, the labor of excavation is extremely difficult, on account of the immense rocks which form a large portion of the soil. Of course, no man can "work out" a "claim" alone. For that reason, and also for the same that makes partnerships desirable, they congregate in companies of four or six, generally designating themselves by the name of the place whence the majority of the members have emigrated; as for example, the "Illinois," "Bunker Hill," "Bay State," etc. companies.

In many places the surface-soil, or in mining-phrase, the "top dirt," "pays" when worked in a "Long Tom." This machine (I have never been able to discover the derivation of its name,) is a trough, generally about twenty feet in length, and eight inches in depth, formed of wood, with the exception of six feet at one end, called the "riddle," (query, why riddle?) which is made of sheet-iron, perforated with holes about the size of a large marble. Underneath this cullender-like portion of the "long-tom," is placed another trough, about ten feet long, the sides six inches perhaps in height, which divided through the middle by a slender slat, is called the "riffle-box."

It takes several persons to manage, properly, a "long-tom." Three or four men station themselves with spades, at the head of the machine, while at the foot of it, stands an individual armed "wid de shovel and de hoe." The spadesmen throw in large quantities of the precious dirt, which is washed down to the "riddle" by a stream of water leading into the "long-tom" through wooden gutters or "sluices." When the soil reaches the "riddle," it is kept constantly in motion by the man with the hoe.

Of course, by this means, all the dirt and gold escapes through the perforations into the "riffle-box" below, one compartment of which is placed just beyond the "riddle." Most of the dirt washes over the sides of the "riffle-box," but the gold being so astonishingly heavy remains safely at the bottom of it.

When the machine gets too full of stones to be worked easily, the man whose business it is to attend to them throws them out with his shovel, looking carefully among them as he does so for any pieces of gold. . . . I am sorry to say that he generally loses his labor. At night they "pan out" the gold, which has been collected in the "riffle-box" during the day.

Many miners decline washing the "top dirt" at all, but try to reach as quickly as possible the "bed-rock," where are found the richest deposits of gold. The river is supposed to have formerly flowed over this "bed-rock," in the "crevices" of which, it left, as it passed away, the largest portions of the so eagerly sought for ore. The group of mountains amidst which we are living is a spur of the Sierra Nevada; and the "bed-rock," (which in this vicinity is of slate) is said to run through the entire range, lying, in distance varying from a few feet to eighty or ninety, beneath the surface of the soil.

On Indian Bar, the "bed-rock" falls in almost perpendicular "benches," while at Rich Bar, the friction of the river has formed it into large, deep basins, in which the gold, instead of being found . . . in the bottom of it, lies for the most part, just below the rim. . . .

When a company wish to reach the bed rock as quickly as possible, they "sink a shaft," (which is nothing more nor less than digging a well,) until they "strike" it. They then commence "drifting coyote holes" (as they call them) in search of "crevices," which, as I told you before, often pay immensely. These "coyote holes" sometimes extend hundreds of feet into the side of the hill.

Of course they are obliged to use lights in working them. They generally proceed, until the air is so impure as to extinguish the lights, when they return to the entrance of the excavation, and commence another, perhaps close to it. When they think that a "coyote hole" has been faithfully "worked," they "clean it up," which is done by scraping the surface of the "bed rock" with a knife,—lest by chance they have overlooked a "crevice,"—and they are often richly rewarded for this precaution.

Now I must tell you how those having "claims" on the hills procure the water for washing them. The expense of raising it in any way from the river, is too enormous to be thought of for a moment. In most cases it is brought from ravines in the mountains. A company, to which a friend of ours belongs, has dug a ditch about a foot in width and depth, and more than three miles in length, which is fed in this way.

I wish that you could see this ditch. I never beheld a NATURAL streamlet more exquisitely beautiful. . . . When it reaches the top of the hill, the sparkling thing is divided into five or six branches, each one of which supplies one, two, or three "long-toms." There is an extra one, called the "waste-ditch," leading to the river, into which the water is shut off at night and on Sundays. This "race" . . . has already cost the company more than five thousand dollars.

They sell the water to others at the following rates: Those that have the first use of it pay ten percent. upon all the gold that they take out. As the water runs off from their machine, (it now goes by the elegant name of "tailings,") it is taken by a company lower down; and as it is not worth so much as when it was clear, the latter pay but seven per cent. If any others wish the "tailings," . . . they pay four percent. on all the gold which they take out. . . . The water companies are constantly in trouble, and the arbitrations on that subject are very frequent. . . .

Gold mining is Nature's great lottery scheme. A man may work in a claim for many months, and be poorer at the end of the time than when he commenced; or he may "take out" thousands in a few hours. . . . It must be acknowledged, however, that if a person "works his claim" himself, is economical and industrious, keeps his health, and is satisfied with small gains, he is "bound" to make money.

And yet . . . almost all with whom we are acquainted seem to have *lost*. Some have had their "claims" jumped; many holes which had been excavated . . . at a great expense, caved in during the heavy rains of the fall and winter. Often after a company has spent an immense deal of time and money in "sinking a shaft," the water from the springs . . . rushes in so fast, that it is impossible to work them. . . .

If a fortunate or unfortunate (which shall I call him?) *does* happen to make a "big strike," he is almost sure to fall into the hands of the professed gamblers, who soon relieve him of all care of it. . . .

Perhaps you would like to know what class of men is most numerous in the mines. As well as I can judge, there are upon this river as many foreigners as Americans. The former, with a few exceptions, are extremely ignorant and degraded; though we have the pleasure of being acquainted with three or four Spaniards of the highest education and accomplishments.

Of the Americans, the majority are of the better class of mechanics. Next to these, in number, are the sailers and the farmers. There are a few merchants and steamboat-clerks, three or four physicians, and one lawyer. We have no ministers, though fourteen miles from here there is a "Rancho," kept by a man of distinguished appearance, an accomplished monte-dealer and horse-jockey, who is *said* to have been—in the States—a preacher of the Gospel. I know not if this be true; but at any rate, such things are not uncommon in California.

THE MULE TRAIN

A picturesque sight in gold rush days was the arrival of a mule train. The Mexican *arriero* (carrier) and his file of small Spanish mules, the mules balancing bulging packs as they wound down a deep gorge, were the miner's life line. Until the twentieth century there was no other way of bringing food and equipment into this wild mining country.

The following selection, describing one such train, is from Louise Clappe's *The Shirley Letters*, first published 1854–55.

May 25,

The very day after I last wrote you, dear M., a troop of mules came on to the Bar, bringing us almost forgotten luxuries, in the form of potatoes, onions and butter. A band of these animals is always a pretty sight, and you can imagine that . . . our having been destitute of the abovementioned edibles since the middle of February, did not detract from the pleasure with which we saw them winding cautiously down the hill, stepping daintily here and there with those absurd little feet of theirs. . . .

They belonged to a Spanish packer; were in excellent condition, sleek and fat as so many kittens, and of every possible color,—black, white, grey, sorrel, cream, brown, etc. Almost all of them had some bit of red, or blue, or yellow, about their trappings, which added not a little to the brilliancy of their appearance; while the gay tinkle of the leader's bell, mingling with those shrill and peculiar exclamations, with which Spanish muleteers are in the habit of urging on their animals, made a not unpleasing medley of sounds.

But the creamiest part of the whole affair was—I must confess it, unromantic as it may seem—when the twenty-five or thirty pretty creatures were collected into the small space between our cabin and the Humboldt [Hotel]; such a gathering together of ham and mackerel-fed bipeds—such a lavish display of gold dust—such troops of happy looking men, bending beneath the delicious weight of butter and potatoes—and above all, *such* a smell of fried onions, as instantaneously rose upon the fragrant California air . . . was, I think, never experienced before.

"JUDGE LYNCH"—FRONTIER LAW

By 1851, the earliest, most lucrative days of the prospector were over. Gold no longer gleamed at the bottom of every mountain stream. Some of the hardest-working miners were replaced by less desirable types. Gamblers with well-worn decks of cards descended on the camps, and crime increased.

Since the only representative of "law and order" was an occasional solitary justice of the peace, without police officers, "Judge Lynch" took over. "The people," who sometimes became an unruly mob, tried and sentenced accused wrongdoers. "Dame Shirley" presented one such episode of frontier justice; her selection concludes with a sentence that may have been remodeled by Bret Harte in a celebrated description in his "Outcasts of Poker Flat."

The selection is from Louise Clappe's *The Shirley Letters*, first published 1854–55.

> *From our Log Cabin, Indian Bar,*
> *December 15, 1851*

I little thought, dear M., that here . . . amid a solitude so grand and lofty that it seems as if the faintest whisper of passion must be hushed by its holy stillness, I should have to relate . . . one of those fearful deeds, which . . . —so utterly at variance with all *civilized* law—must make our beautiful California appear to strangers rather as a hideous phantom, than the flower-wreathed reality which she is. . . .

The facts in this sad case are as follows: Last fall, two men were arrested by their partners, on suspicion of having stolen from them eighteen hundred dollars in gold dust. The evidence was not sufficient to convict them, and they were acquitted. They were tried before a meeting of the miners—as at that time the law did not even *pretend* to wave its scepter over this place.

The prosecutors still believed them guilty, and fancied that the gold was hidden in a "coyote hole," near the camp from which it had been taken. They therefore watched the place narrowly while the suspected men remained on the Bar. They made no discoveries, however; and soon after the trial, the acquitted persons left the mountains for Marysville.

A few weeks ago, one of these men returned, and has spent most of the time since his arrival in . . . the different bar-rooms upon the river. . . . As soon as the losers of the gold heard of his return, they bethought themselves of the "coyote hole," and placed about its entrance some brushwood and stones, in such a manner that no one could go into it without disturbing the arrangement of them. In the meanwhile the thief settled at Rich Bar. . . .

A few mornings ago, he returned to his boarding place . . . with a spade in his hand, and . . . carelessly observed that he had "been out prospecting." The losers of the gold went, immediately after breakfast . . . to see if all was right at the "coyote hole." On this fatal day, they saw that the entrance had been disturbed, and going in, they found upon the ground, a money belt which had apparently just been cut open.

Armed with this evidence of guilt, they confronted the suspected person and sternly accused him of having the gold in his possession. . . . He did not attempt a denial, but said that if they would not bring him to a trial, (which of course they promised) he would give it up immediately. He then informed them that they would find it beneath the blankets of his *bunk*. . . . There, sure enough, were six hundred dollars of the missing money, and the unfortunate wretch declared that his partner had taken the remainder to the States.

By this time the exciting news had spread all over the Bar. A meeting of the miners was immediately convened, the unhappy man was taken into custody, a jury chosen, and a judge, lawyer, etc., appointed. Whether the men, who had just regained a portion of their missing property, made any objections . . . I know not; if they had done so, however, it would have made no difference, as the *people* had taken the matter entirely out of their hands.

At one o'clock, so rapidly was the trial conducted,

the judge charged the jury, and gently insinuated that they could do no less than to bring in with their verdict of guilty, a sentence of *death*! . . . After a few minutes' absence, the twelve men who had consented to burden their souls with a responsibility so fearful, returned, and the foreman handed to the judge a paper, from which he read the will of the *people*, as follows: "That William Brown, convicted of stealing, etc., should, in *one hour* from that time, be hung by the neck until he was dead."

By the persuasions of some men more mildly disposed, they granted him a respite of *three hours*. . . . He employed the time in writing in his native language (he is a Swede) to some friends in Stockholm; God help them when that fatal post shall arrive. . . . He had exhibited during the trial, the utmost recklessness . . . and when the rope was placed about his neck, was evidently much intoxicated. All at once, however, he seemed startled into a consciousness of . . . his position, and requested a few moments for prayer.

The execution was conducted by the jury, and was performed by throwing the cord, one end of which was attached to the neck of the prisoner, across the limb of a tree standing outside of the Rich Bar graveyard; when all, who felt disposed to engage in so revolting a task, lifted the poor wretch from the ground, in the most awkward manner possible. The whole affair, indeed, was a piece of cruel butchery. . . .

It is said that the crowd generally, seemed to feel the solemnity of the occasion; but many of the drunkards, who form a large part of the community on these Bars, laughed and shouted, as if it were a spectacle got up for their particular amusement. A disgusting specimen of intoxicated humanity . . . staggered up to the victim, who was praying at the moment, and crowding a dirty rag into his almost unconscious hand . . . tearfully implored him to take his "hankercher," and if he were *innocent* . . . to drop it as soon as he was drawn up into the air, but if *guilty*, not to let it fall on any account.

The body of the criminal was allowed to hang for some hours after the execution. It had commenced storming in the earlier part of the evening; and when those, whose business it was to inter the remains, arrived at the spot, they found them enwrapped in a soft white shroud of feathery snow-flakes, as if pitying Nature had tried to hide from the offended face of heaven, the cruel deed which her mountain children had committed.

SECOND-CLASS CITIZENS

In the rush for gold, many common decencies were trampled. In San Francisco hospitals the sick were left without change of bedclothes or proper nursing. In San Francisco Harbor, around 500 ships floated about abandoned, their crews having been lured to the mountains by the feverish vision of gold. Soldiers deserted garrisons, and jailers transported their prisoners to the high Sierra —where the prisoners could help the jailers prospect for gold.

Among other casualties of the gold rush was General Kearny's pledge, given in 1847, that Americans would respect the civil rights of Spanish-speaking Californians (see p. 157). Instead of respecting these rights, the newcomers often flouted them.

"Foreigners," especially Mexican-Americans, were resented, and sometimes expelled from the mines. The state legislature taxed them for the privilege of working in the diggings—where they were frequently taken advantage of. Fights were common, and the killing of a Mexican-American created little stir.

"Dame Shirley" recorded several instances of this prejudice and unfair treatment, which has been called "one of the darkest threads in the fabric of Anglo-Saxon frontier government." The episodes described below are from her Letters 14, 16, 18, and 19. The selection is from Louise Clappe's *The Shirley Letters*, first published 1854–55.

From our Log Cabin, Indian Bar,
March 15, 1852

Nothing is more amusing, than to observe the different styles, in which the generality of the Americans talk *at* the unfortunate Spaniard. In the first place, many of them really believe, that when they have learned *sabe* and *vamos*, (two words which they seldom use in the right place,) *poco tiempo, si,* and *bueno* . . . they have the whole of the glorious Castilian at their tongue's end.

Some, however . . . fancy, that by . . . screaming forth their sentences in good solid English, they can be surely understood; others . . . make the most excruciatingly grotesque gesture. . . . The majority, however, place a . . . touching faith in *broken English,* and when they murder it, with the few words of Castilian quoted above, are firmly convinced, that it is nothing but their "ugly dispositions" which makes the Spaniards pretend not to understand them.

One of those dear, stupid Yankees . . . was relating *his* experience . . . the other day. . . . He had lost a horse somewhere among the hills, and during his search for it, met a gentlemanly Chileno, who . . . made the most desperate efforts to understand the questions put to him. Of course, *Chileno* was so stupid that he did not succeed, for it is not possible that one of the "Great American People" could fail to express himself clearly. . . . Our Yankee friend . . . declared that he [the *Chileno*] only "played possum from sheer *ugliness*."

"Why," he added . . . "the cross, old rascal pretended not to understand his own language, though I said as plainly as possible '*Señor, sabe mi horso vamos poco tempo?*' [Sir, you know my? we go little time] which, perhaps you don't know," he proceeded to say . . . "means, 'Sir, I have lost my horse, have you seen it?' "

I am ashamed to acknowledge, that we did *not* know the above written Anglo-Spanish sentence to mean *that*! The honest fellow concluded . . . "They ain't kinder like *eour* [*sic*] folks."

From our Log Cabin, Indian Bar,
May 1, 1852

A few evenings ago, a Spaniard was stabbed by an American. It seems that the presumptuous foreigner had the impertinence, to ask very humbly and meekly that most noble representative of the stars and stripes, if the latter would pay him a few dollars which he had owed him for some time. . . . The poor Spaniard received, for answer, several inches of cold steel in his breast, which inflicted a very dangerous wound. Nothing was done, and very little was said about this atrocious affair.

At Rich Bar they have passed a set of resolutions for . . . the summer; one of which is . . . that no foreigner shall work in the mines on the Bar. This has caused nearly all the Spaniards to immigrate upon Indian Bar, and several new houses for the sale of liquor etc., are building by these people. It seems to me that the above law is selfish, cruel and narrow-minded in the extreme.

From our Log Cabin, Indian Bar,
July 5, 1852

About five o'clock, we arrived at home, just in time to hear some noisy shouts of "Down with the Spaniards;" "The great American People forever," and other similar cries, evident signs of quite a spirited fight between the two parties, which was, in reality, taking place at the moment. Seven or eight of the *elite* of Rich Bar, drunk with whisky and patriotism, were the principal actors in this unhappy affair, which resulted in serious injury to two or three Spaniards.

For some time past, there has been a gradually increasing state of bad feeling exhibited by our countrymen (increased, we fancy, by the ill-treatment which our Consul received the other day at Acapulco,) towards foreigners. In this affair, our own countrymen were principally to blame, or, rather I should say, Sir Barley Corn was to blame, for many of the ringleaders are fine young men, who, when sober, are decidedly friendly to the Spaniards.

From our Log Cabin, Indian Bar,
August 4, 1852

In a *melé* [sic] between the Americans and the foreigners, Domingo—a tall, majestic-looking Spaniard, a perfect type of the novelistic bandit of Old Spain—had stabbed Tom Somers, a young Irishman, but a naturalized citizen of the United States. . . . When Tom Somers fell, the Americans, being unarmed, were seized with a sudden panic and fled. There was a rumor, (unfounded, as it afterwards proved) to the effect, that the Spaniards had on this day conspired to kill all the Americans on the river.

In a few moments, however, the latter rallied and made a rush at the murderer, who immediately plunged into the river and . . . escaped. . . .

In the meanwhile, the consternation was terrific. The Spaniards, who, with the exception of six or eight, knew no more of the affair than I did, thought that the Americans had arisen against them; and our own countrymen . . . fancied the same of the foreigners. About twenty of the latter, who were either sleeping or reading in their cabins at the time of the *émeute* [riot], aroused by the cry of "Down with the Spaniards!" barricaded themselves in a drinking-saloon, determined to defend themselves as long as possible against the massacre, which was fully expected. . . .

In the bake-shop, which stands next door to our cabin, young Tom Somers lay straightened for the grave . . . while over his dead body a Spanish woman, was weeping and moaning in the most piteous and heart-rending manner.

The Rich Barians, who had heard a most exaggerated account of the rising of the Spaniards against the Americans, armed with rifles, pistols, clubs, dirks, etc., were rushing down the hill by hundreds. Each one added fuel to his rage, by crowding into the little bakery, to gaze upon the blood-bathed bosom of the victim. . . .

Then arose the most fearful shouts of "Down with the Spaniards!" "Drive every foreigner off the river!" "Don't let one of the murderous devils remain." . . .

After a time, the more sensible and sober part of the community succeeded in quieting, in a partial degree, the enraged and excited multitude.

A MEXICAN-AMERICAN VIEW

One Spanish-speaking Californian who took part in politics after the American occupation, and who was respected by all, was General Mariano Guadalupe Vallejo.

Vallejo, "Commandante of the Line of the North" under Mexican rule, had been a leading progressive. He had helped many American emigrants who arrived gaunt and exhausted from their trek across the plains. He believed that American expansion to California was inevitable and even hoped that United States rule might be an improvement over Mexican turmoil—but he was disappointed.

Toward the end of his career, Vallejo wrote a history of California, in which he told how it felt to become a second-class citizen. The following selection is from Vallejo's "What the Gold Rush Brought to California" (from his *History*, as printed in Valeska Bari, *The Course of Empire*).

When gold was discovered, the flag of stars already waved above Alta California. No longer were we ruled by the Mexican laws, under whose shadow some had advanced while others fell back, but under which no one had perished of hunger, and only two individuals had been by law deprived of their lives, a very common event during the early years of the North American domination in California.

The language now spoken in our country, the laws which govern us, the faces which we encounter daily, are those of the masters of the land, and of course antagonistic to our interests and rights, but what does that matter to the conqueror? He wishes his own well-being and not ours!—a thing that I consider only natural in individuals, but which I condemn in a government which has promised to respect and make respected our rights, and to treat us as its own sons. But what does it avail us to complain?.... There is no remedy.

Although the treaty of Guadalupe Hidalgo imposed on the North Americans an obligation to respect established rights, the Americans, always astute and filled with cunning, placed the owners of valuable lands in such a position that they often saw themselves obliged to expend the value of their properties to obtain valid titles to them. There were times when, after obtaining in San Francisco, at great cost, a favorable verdict in the federal courts . . . an order, issued to favor some protégé, would come from Washington that the case must be reviewed by the Supreme Court . . . in which tribunal the California owner was almost certain to lose his lands.

This method of procedure was not in harmony with the honeyed words of the American orators. . . .

In my humble opinion the change of government which took place in California . . . has resulted in benefit to the commerce and agriculture of the young state, but in damage to the morale of the people, whose patriarchal customs have broken down little by little through contact with so many immoral persons who came to this my country from every nook and corner of the known world. A great part of the blame . . . can rightly be attributed to the state and federal government. . . .

I assert that, in carrying out of the treaty of Guadalupe Hidalgo, the North Americans have treated the Californians as a conquered people and not as citizens who voluntarily joined to form part of the great family dwelling beneath the glorious flag which flamed so proudly from Bunker Hill.

7

The Thirty-first State

This is a great day for California!
—Johann Augustus Sutter

Procession celebrating statehood

TRANSITION

The "California Fever"—the rush to the gold mines—peopled California with Anglo-Saxons and laid the foundations of its industry and commerce. But a fever cannot last forever. When all the likely streams had been searched and large corporations had to take over the hunt for rifts too deep for the lone prospector to work, what would the immigrants turn to?

As early as 1849 the brisk Vermonter Walter Colton made some conjectures about California's future. He discussed other ways of making a living, the chances for slavery in California, and the dangers to Spanish land titles from the newcomers.

The following selection, in which Colton proved himself a true prophet, is from Walter Colton's *Three Years in California* (1850).

WEDNESDAY, MARCH 7, 1848.

Emigrants, when the phrensy [sic] of the mines has passed, will be strongly attracted to Los Angeles, the capital of the southern department. It stands inland from San Pedro about eight leagues, in the bosom of a broad fertile plain, and has a population of two thousand souls. The San Gabriel pours its sparkling tide through its green borders. The most delicious fruits of the tropical zone may flourish here.

As yet, only the grape and fig have secured the

attention of the cultivator; but the capacities of the soil and aptitudes of the climate are attested in the twenty thousand vines, which reel in one orchard, and which send through California a wine that need not blush in the presence of any rival from the hills of France or the sunny slopes of Italy. To these plains the more quiet emigrants will ere long gather, and convert their drills into pruning-hooks, and we shall have wines, figs, dates, almonds, olives, and raisins from California. The gold may give out, but these are secure while nature remains.

San Diego is another spot to which the tide of immigration must turn. It stands on the border line of Alta California, and opens on a land-locked bay of surpassing beauty. The climate is soft and mild the year round; the sky brilliant, and the atmosphere free of those mists which the cold currents throw on the northern sections of the coast. . . . I would rather have a willow-wove hut at San Diego, with ground enough for a garden, than the whole peninsula of San Francisco, if I must live there. The one is Vallambrosa, where only the zephyr stirs her light wing; the other a tempest-swept cave of Aeolus, where the demons of storm shake their shivering victims. . . . San Diego will . . . become the queen of the south in California, encircled with vineyards and fields of golden grain.

TUESDAY, MARCH 20, 1848.

The land-titles in California ought to receive the most indulgent construction. But few of them have *all* the forms prescribed by legislative enactments, but they have official insignia sufficient to certify the intentions of the government. To disturb these grants would be alike impolitic and unjust; it would be to convert the lands which they cover to the public domain, and ultimately turn them over to speculators and foreign capitalists. Better let them remain as they are: they are now in good hands; they are held mostly by Californians,—a class of persons who part with them on reasonable terms.

No Californian grinds the face of the poor, or refuses an emigrant a participation in his lands. I have seen them dispose of miles for a consideration less than would be required by Americans for as many acres. You are shut up to the shrewdness and sharpness of the Yankee on the one hand, and the liberality of the Californian on the other. Your choice lies between the two and I have no hesitation in saying, give me the Californian.

If he has a farm, and I have none, he will divide with me; but who ever heard of a Yankee splitting up his farm to accommodate emigrants? Why, he will not divide with his own sons till death has divided him from both. Yankees are good when mountains are to be levelled, lakes drained, and lightning converted into a vegetable manure; but as a landholder, deliver me from his map and maw.

WEDNESDAY, JUNE 20, 1848.

The causes which exclude slavery from California lie within a nut-shell. All here are diggers, and free white diggers wont dig with slaves. They know they must dig themselves: they have come out here for that purpose, and they wont degrade their calling by associating it with slave-labor. . . .

An army of half a million, backed by the resources of the United States, could not shake their purpose. Of all men with whom I have ever met, the most firm, resolute, and indomitable, are the emigrants into California. They feel that they have got into a new world, where they have a right to shape and settle things in their own way. . . . They may offer to come into the Union, but they consider it an act of condescension.

THE THIRTY-FIRST STAR

California is one of the few states which entered the Union as an "instant state"—without ever having been organized as a territory. Restless, independent miners were not going to be governed by officials sent out from Washington; they were going to govern themselves. They pressured General Bennett Riley, military governor of California, to call a constitutional convention, which met at Sacramento in the fall of 1849. The convention elected Dr. Robert Semple, a covered-wagon pioneer, as its president. Then it adopted a constitution containing the latest reforms and prohibiting slavery on California soil. Californians at once ratified the constitution and sent two Senators, John Charles Frémont and William M. Gwin, knocking at the doors of Congress.

Bayard Taylor, world traveler and scholar who visited California in 1849, sensed the spirit of the constitutional convention. He found California "the most democratic country in the world" because here, where "lawyers, physicians and ex-professors" swung pickaxes, "LABOR IS RESPECTABLE." The following selection, describing the constitutional convention, is from Bayard Taylor's *El Dorado* (1850).

The building in which the Convention met [at Monterey] in September, 1849, to draft a State Constitution was probably the only one in California suited to the purpose. It is a handsome, two-story edifice of yellow sandstone situated on a gentle slope above the town. It is named "Colton Hall," on account of its having been built by Don Walter Colton, former Alcalde of Monterey, from the proceeds of a sale of city lots. . . .

The upper story, in which the Convention sat, formed a single hall about sixty feet in length by twenty-five in breadth. A railing running across the middle divided the members from the spectators. The former were seated at four long tables, the President occupying a rostrum at the further end, over which were suspended two American flags and an extraordinary picture of Washington. . . .

The Declaration of Rights, which was the first subject before the Convention, occasioned little discussion. Its sections . . . were nearly all adopted by unanimous vote. The clause prohibiting slavery was met by no word of dissent; it was the universal sentiment of the Convention. . . . The election of judges by the people—the right of married women to property—the establishment of a liberal system of education—and other reforms . . . were all transplanted to the . . . Pacific Coast.

The Articles of the Constitution relating to the Executive, Judicial and Legislative Departments occupied several days, but the debates were dry and uninteresting. . . . A section being before the Convention declaring that every citizen arrested for a criminal offense would be tried by a jury of his peers, a member unfamiliar with such technical terms moved to strike out the word "peers." "I don't like the word 'peers,' " said he; "it ain't republican; I'd like to know what we want with *peers* in this country—we're not a monarchy. . . . I vote for no such law."

The boundary question, however, . . . assumed a character of real interest and importance. The great point of dispute . . . was the eastern limit of the State.

... When [a final compromise] came to be designated on the map, most of the members were better satisfied than they had anticipated. They had a State with eight hundred miles of seacoast and an average of two hundred and fifty miles in breadth, including both sides of the Sierra Nevada. ...

About one o'clock [October 13] the Convention met again; few of the members, indeed, had left the hall [after the morning session]. ... They proceeded to affix their names to the completed Constitution. At this moment a signal was given; the American colors ran up the flagstaff in front of the Government buildings ... the first gun boomed from the fort.

All the native enthusiasm of Captain Sutter's Swiss blood was aroused. ... He sprang from his seat and, waving his hand around his head as if swinging a sword, exclaimed: "Gentlemen, this is the happiest day of my life. It makes me glad to hear those cannon; they remind me of the time I was a soldier. Yes, I am glad to hear them—this is a great day for California!" Then ... he sat down, the tears streaming from his eyes.

The members ... gave three tumultuous cheers. ... Gun followed gun from the fort ... till finally as the loud ring of the *thirty-first* was heard, there was a shout: "That's for California!" and everyone joined in giving three times three for the new star added to our Confederation.

Southerners did not wish California to come into the Union as a free state, but Senator Henry Clay, of Kentucky, persuaded them to accept California in return for the North's promising to send runaway slaves back to their owners in the South. As a result of "Clay's Compromise," Congress passed the "Act for the Admission of California into the Union ... September 9, 1850."

Epilogue

When California entered the Union, the most romantic period of its history came to an end. It was no longer a glittering pawn on the international chessboard, a prize for the taking. The less glamorous immigrants after 1850 included salesmen with carpetbags, hard-luck farmers, and retired businessmen from the snowy Middle West. Perhaps the thousands of pigtailed Chinese laborers who arrived to work on the railroads were the most picturesque of the latecomers.

Yet this thirty-first state, "physically, one of the most remarkable . . . of the Union," continued to haunt the dreams of many. It played a role of growing importance in the affairs of the nation and began to tilt the balance of population, wealth, and innovation westward.

During the Civil War the free state of California was the Pacific anchor of the Union. Too distant to give effective military aid, it provided only a few enthusiastic volunteers—but indispensable financial strength through its gold. Supporters of the Union defeated a movement to make California a "Pacific Republic," independent of both North and South. And leaders, in the state and in the nation, came at last to realize the absolute necessity of linking East and West by a transcontinental railroad. They saw that the natural cleavage of the United States is not along an imaginary Mason-Dixon line but north and south along the Rocky Mountains or the Sierra Nevada.

So Congress adopted the central route to California and the tracks were laid. On May 10, 1869, rails built eastward from Sacramento were joined, in Utah, to rails built westward from Omaha by a "Golden Spike." California's centuries-old isolation was at an end.

Even before this dramatic event, transportation had been one of the young state's more exciting new industries. In 1858, John Butterfield had begun to operate his cross-continent stagecoaches, the Overland Mail Company. Polished Concord coaches, serviced by 1,000 men, made the run from St. Louis to San Francisco by the southern (New Mexico) route in twenty four days. In 1860 the legendary Pony Express was inaugurated, and its riders—"swift phantoms of the desert," Mark Twain called them—cut the time to ten days. However, the gossamer wire of the first telegraph to the West Coast, stretched over prairie and mountain in 1861, had ended the Pony Express.

More prosaic, perhaps, but not without their adventurous aspects were the traditional cattle raising, sheep raising, and wheat farming. For a while, the *Californios* retained ownership of their vast ranches on the brown hills and "sunburned rivers" of the south and enjoyed a boom. The price of beef skyrocketed because of the miners' need for food.

Then the Federal Land Act of 1851, requiring all landowners to submit their titles for examination, led to the gradual displacement of many *Californios* by Yankees—just as Walter Colton had feared. Sheep raising now became as profitable as cattle raising, to the disgust of the great conservationist John Muir, who was to explore and save Yosemite Valley for the people. (Sheep are the most efficient lawn mowers ever invented; they devastated fields and beautiful upland meadows, to Muir's dismay.)

A little later, wheat farming was the chief road to wealth. The wheat was grown on great estates, "factories in the fields" owned by a few wealthy operators and cultivated with cheap labor. "Specialty crops"—citrus fruits, nuts, avocados, lettuce, cotton, tomatoes, grapes—were also introduced or developed and helped make California the leading agricultural state in the Union. But these crops, too, were produced on large holdings cultivated by cheap labor. The underpaid workers—Japanese, Chinese, later "Okies" and Mexicans—created a social problem which still troubles California.

Gold, cattle, sheep, wheat, oranges; in the twentieth century, movies, oil, and the aerospace industry—California has been a cornucopia whose outpouring a somewhat dazed American Republic is still trying to evaluate. California has also, for more than a hundred years, served as one of the last frontiers for Americans. It has offered a second chance—high wages or profits, open space, an opportunity for a better life in the western sunshine.

That dream of the earthly paradise is not dead today, in spite of crowded freeways and problems of ecology. It lives on even while California, our window on the Pacific, finds itself battered by the great tides of expanding world trade, population growth, and Third World conflict. Formed by titanic earthquakes of ages past, invaded by emissaries of God and Satan—peaceful Indians, friars, ranchers, gamblers, highwaymen, forty-niners, fur traders, land speculators—California yet retains something of the aura of mystery with which Ordóñez de Montalvo endowed his imagined province. What the poet Robert Frost felt nearly a century ago in San Francisco may still be felt in that famous city, in the high Sierra, or on the wide desert:

> Dust always blowing about the town,
> Except when sea fog laid it down,
> And I was one of the children told
> Some of the blowing dust was gold.

A Timetable of Events

30,000 B.C. (?) Brown-skinned men from Asia cross the Bering land bridge to Alaska, then journey south to California.

1542–43 Juan Rodríguez Cabrillo becomes the first European to explore the California coast; his two ships reach southern Oregon.

1579 Francis Drake lands in northern California, names it Nova Albion, and claims it for Queen Elizabeth I.

1602–03 Sebastián Vizcaíno sails back over Cabrillo's route, discovers Monterey, and gives many places their modern names.

1769 Gaspar de Portolá makes the first Spanish settlement, at San Diego, and marches north to San Francisco Bay.

1769–1823 Fray Junípero Serra and his successors found twenty-one Franciscan missions, from San Diego to Sonoma, to convert and pacify the Indians.

1774–75 Juan Bautista de Anza opens a land route from Sonora, Mexico, through Arizona, to southern California.

1775 The Indians at San Diego revolt and kill one friar but are put to flight.

1781 Yuma Indians massacre Spanish emigrants and destroy missions on the Colorado River, thus closing Anza's land route to California.

1806 Nikolai Rezanov, Russian diplomat, lands at San Francisco to reconnoiter but falls in love with the daughter of the Spanish commandant.

1812 Ivan Kuskov comes to California from Alaska and builds Fort Ross, a Russian base, just north of San Francisco.

1822 Spanish rule ends; California pledges allegiance to Mexico, which has just won independence from Spain.

1826	Jedediah Smith leads the first party of American trappers overland from Utah to San Gabriel Mission, near Los Angeles.
1833	The Mexican government secularizes the Franciscan missions; speculators and ranchers get control of the land, which was supposed to return to the Indians.
1834–36	Richard Henry Dana voyages from Boston around Cape Horn, takes part in California coastal trade, and gathers material for his *Two Years Before the Mast*.
1839–40	Johann Augustus Sutter obtains 50,000 acres near the Sacramento River, builds a "Fort," and protects Americans settling there.
1841	The Russians abandon Fort Ross because of heavy expenses; they sell the movable property to Johann Augustus Sutter.
1844	John C. Frémont leads a U.S. government expedition over the Sierra Nevada to the Sacramento Valley and maps the route for future settlers.
1846	The "Bear Flaggers"—trappers and settlers on the Sacramento—revolt against Mexican officials and establish an independent "California Republic."
1846	The United States declares war on Mexico; the U.S. Navy occupies California ports from San Francisco to San Diego.
1848	The Treaty of Guadalupe Hidalgo ends the Mexican-American War and gives California, New Mexico, and Arizona to the United States.
1848	James Marshall finds gold in the American River; the resulting gold rush increases the non-Indian population of California from 26,000 to 115,000 in one year.
1849	A popularly elected convention meets at Monterey and drafts a constitution for California.
1850	Congress admits California to the Union as the thirty-first state.

Books About the History of California

CAUGHEY, JOHN W., *Gold Is the Cornerstone*. Berkeley, University of California Press, 1948. An excellent survey of the era of the Gold Rush.

CHAPMAN, CHARLES E., *A History of California: The Spanish Period*. New York, Macmillan Company, 1921. A sympathetic account of the Spanish settlement—early explorers and the pastoral period.

CHEVIGNY, HECTOR, *Russian America*. New York, Viking Press, 1965. The best narrative of the Russian advance to Alaska and the West Coast.

CLELAND, ROBERT GLASS, *From Wilderness to Empire*. New York, Alfred A. Knopf, 1959. A readable history of California, particularly valuable for the later nineteenth century.

LEE, W. STORRS, *California: A Literary Chronicle*. New York, Funk & Wagnalls, 1968. A well-chosen anthology of writings about California, from Juan Rodríguez Cabrillo to Robinson Jeffers.

McWILLIAMS, CAREY, ed., *The California Revolution*. New York, Grossman Publishers, 1968. A provocative collection of essays about new life-styles in contemporary California.

MAYNARD, THEODORE, *The Long Road of Father Serra*. New York, Appleton-Century-Crofts, 1954. Popular biography of the most popular figure of the California missions.

POURADE, RICHARD F., *The Call to California*. San Diego, Union-Tribune Publishing Company, 1968. The Portolá expedition and first Spanish settlement of California, with picture-story illustrations.

RIESENBERG, FELIX, *The Golden Road*. New York, McGraw-Hill Book Company, Inc., 1962. The fascinating story of the coast road (*El Camino Real*), its rogues and rancheros, friars and fortyniners.

ROLLE, ANDREW F., *California: A History*. New York, Thomas Y. Crowell Company, 1963. The best general history of California, with excellent bibliographies at the end of each chapter.

(*For sources of contemporary writings about early California, see the introductions to the selections in this book.*)

Index

"Amazons," 19–21
American Civil War, 214, 215
American River, 126–29, 163
  prospecting on, 170 ff.
Anian, Strait of, 21–22, 35, 44
Anson, George, 46, 51
Anza, Juan Bautistaple, 70, 77
Argüello, Concepción, 83–89, 93, 104
Argüello, Don Luis, 83
Arillaga, José, 83
Army of the West, 145
Ascensión, Antonio dé la, 41 ff.
Atherton, Gertrude, 84

Beale, Lt., 147
Bailey, Nancy Ann, 185–87
Bancroft, George, 135 ff.
"Battle of the Old Woman's Gun," 145
Bear Flag Revolt, 136–39
Bering, Vitus, 51, 81, 90
Bering Strait, 81
Bidwell, John, 121
Bodega Bay, 94, 96, 98
Boom towns, 176. See also Marysville
Bouchard, Hippolyte de, 105
Bradshaw, John, 110–11
Brannan, Sam, 166
Buriel, Andrés, 46
Butterfield, John, 216

Cabrillo, Juan Rodríguez, 22–29
California. See also specific entries
  climate, 12–13
  formation, 11–13
  geographical misconceptions, 19 ff., 45
  name, origin of, 19–21
  size, 11
California Battalion, 163
Californios, 117, 136, 140 ff., 216

  revolt of, 144 ff.
  treatment of, 157–59
Cape Horn, 111, 167
Carillo, José Antonio, 145
Castro, José, 145
Catholic Church. See Missionaries
Cavendish, Thomas, 40
Central Valley, 12, 106
Cermêno, Sebastian, 40
Chinese laborers, 215
Clappe, Louise ("Dame Shirley"), 180 ff.
Clay, Henry, 214
Clipper ships, 111–18
Coast Range Mountains, 11–13
Coloma, California, 163
Colorado Desert, 14, 106–9
Colorado River, 21, 71
Colton, Walter, 167, 168, 209–11, 213, 216
Columbus, Christopher, 19–21
Constitution (of California), 212–14
Constitutional Convention, 213
Coronedo, Vásquez de, 22
Cortés, Hernando, 21–22
Costansó, Miguel, 54, 62
Crespi, Father, 59, 66

Dana, Richard Henry, 112–21
Davis, William Heath, 124
Downey, Joseph T., 139–40, 149, 151, 153
Drake, Francis, 34–36, 40

Explorations, 21 ff.
Elizabeth I, 35–36
Emory, William, 157

Farming, present, 12–14, 209–10
Feather River, 176 ff.
Fernández, Juan, 167
Ferrelo, Bartolomé, 29

221

Field, Stephen, 176
Flores, José María, 144, 153, 157
Food, 173 ff.
  costs, 173, 176
  diet, 173
  staples, scarcity of, 173, 176, 194, 195
Fort Ross, 93–99, 124
Forty-niners, 167 ff. *See also* Gold rush (of '49)
  kinds of people, 167–69, 193–94
  life-style, 179, 182 ff.
Franciscans, 12, 51 ff., 166
Frederick VII, 45
Frémont, John Charles, 101, 121–28, 136, 138, 141, 143, 212
Frontier law, 120, 180, 195 ff., 201
Frost, Robert, 217

Galvéz, José de, 47, 53
Gillespie, Archibald, 144–48
Gold, 164 ff.
  after 1851, 195 ff.
  claims, 173, 189, 190
  depletion of, 209, 240
  discovery of, 164–66
  extent of, 195 ff.
Gold rush (of '49), 163 ff. *See also* Food; Forty-niners; Gold; Mining communities; Prospecting
Golden Gate, 12
Golden Hind, 34–35
Gómez, Father, 59, 66
Great Britain, exploration of California, 34–38, 40
Greek Church, 96–97
Greeley, Horace, 134, 167
Gulf of California, 22, 45
Gwin, William M., 212

Hakluyt, Richard, 17
Hammond, Lt. 147
Harte, Bret, 181, 196
Herodotus, 19

Independence, Missouri, 121–29
Indians, 14, 20, 24–27, 31, 42–43, 56, 59, 64, 69 ff., 96–98, 107, 119, 123–26, 134, 142, 163
  Apache, 46
  Aztec, 21
  Digger, 107
  meet Cabrillo, 24–27
  mission, 166
  with missionaries, 69 ff.
  with Sutter, 123–26
  Yuma, 71
Iturbide, Augustín de, 105

Jiménez, Fortún, 21
"Judge Lynch," 195 ff. *See also* Frontier law

Kearny, Stephen W., 145–49, 151, 153–57
Kings Highway, 12
Koskov, Ivan, 94
Kotzebue, Otto von, 94

Langsdorff, Georg von, 83–84, 87, 93–94
Larkin, Thomas, 136
Law. *See* Frontier law; "Judge Lynch"
"Long Tom," 190–91
Los Angeles (Pueblo de los Angeles), 26, 106, 120, 141–45, 149 ff., 209
  march to, 149–57
"Luck of Roaring Camp, The" (Harte), 185

MacRae, Archibald, 141–43
"Manifest Destiny," 134
Marshall, James, 163–66
Marysville, California, 176–78, 184, 196
Mendoza, Antonio de, 22
Merritt, Ezekiel, 136
Mexico, 134, 170
  relations with United States, 134–35, 139
  under Spanish rule, 21
Mexican-American War, 132 ff., 163
  1845, 134–35
  1846, 136–53. *See also* Bear Flag Revolt
  1847, 153–59
Mexican-Americans, 199–203
Mexican Civil War, 104–5, 163
Mining communities, 180 ff.
  cabins, description of, 181, 183–85
  funeral, 185–87
  hotel, description of, 181–82, 187–88
Missionaries, 46, 51 ff.
Missions, 59, 68–69, 75, 96
  decline of, 118 ff.
Monterey, 41–42, 68–69
Montezuma, 21
Montalvo, Ordóñez de, 19–21, 45, 181, 217
Montgomery, John B., 139
Mormons, 134, 145–46, 165–66
Mule trains, 194–95
Muir, John, 216

Napoleon, 104
New York *Tribune*, 134, 167
Noticia de la California (Burriel), 46
"Nova Albion," 34–36

222

Okun, S. B., 91 ff.
Onate, Juan de, 46
Oregon, 23, 94, 106
"Outcasts of Poker Flat" (Harte), 196
Ortega, José, 66–67

Palou, Francisco, 51 ff.
Pattie, James O., 106–11
Philippine Islands, 36, 42, 46, 62
Pico, Andrés, 146 ff.
Polk, James K., 135, 158, 167
Pony Express, 216
Population, 167
Port Romanzow, 96
Portolá, Gaspar de, 54 ff.
Proclamation to the People of California, 157–59
Prospecting, 169 ff.
  methods, 171, 190–92
  profits, 172–73, 190–93

Railroads, 215–16
Rezanov, Nikolai, 79, 82–93, 104
Rezanov, (Atherton), 84 ff.
Riley, Bennett, 212
Russia, interest in California, 81 ff.
Russian-American Company, 82, 91, 97

Sacramento River, 12, 123, 126, 128–29, 177
Salinas Valley, 136
Salvatierra, Juan María, 46
San Andreas Fault, 14
San Catalina Mission, 106, 109
San Francisco (Yerba Buena), 12–14, 94, 99, 136 ff., 180 ff., 199, 205, 210
  discovery of San Francisco Bay, 66–71
Solano Mission, 96
San Diego, 12–13, 25, 106, 109, 141 ff., 210
San Gabriel, 96, 120
  Mission, 74, 106
  River, 153–54, 209

San Miguel, 26, 29
San Pascual, Battle of, 145
San Pedro, 121, 141–42, 145
San Salvador, 22–26
Semple, Robert, 212
Sergas de Esplanadían (Montalvo), 19
Serra, Junípero, 51 ff.
Seven Cities of Cíbola, 22
Sierra Nevada, 11–13, 28, 121–23
Slavery, 211–15
Sloat, John D., 132, 135, 139
Smith, Jedediah, 105 ff.
Spain, interest in California, 21 ff., 104
Sutter, Johann Augustus, 99 ff., 123 ff., 163 ff., 214
Sutter's Fort (New Helvetia), 123–24, 127, 136, 163–65

Taylor, Bayard, 212
Telegraph service, 216
Texas, 134, 138
Transportation (49'ers), 167–68
Treaty of Guadalupe-Hidalgo (1848), 157, 204–5
Twain, Mark, 216
Two Years Before the Mast (Dana), 113

Ulloa, Francisco de, 22
U.S. government, interest in California, 132 ff.
U. S. Navy, 132 ff.
  involvement in California, 134 ff.
  Proclamation (1846), 132, 140
Urdenata, Andrés de, 36 ff.

Vallejo, Mariano, 136–38, 203–4
Victoria, 22, 27–28
Vizcaíno, Sebastian, 40 ff., 60–62

Woods, Daniel, 170
Women settlers, 167–69, 180, 185. *See also* Clappe, Louise

Yankees, 99, 105 ff.
Yuba River, 169

Photo Credits

Bancroft Library, University of California at Berkeley, 8–9, 50 (bottom), 79, 131, 133, 174 (top), 207, 208

California Redwood Association, 2, 80

National Park Service, 17, 102

Santa Fe Railroad, 174 (bottom)

Southern Pacific Railroad, 161, 175

Title Trust and Insurance Company of Los Angeles, 18, 49, 50 (top), 101, 103 (top), 132, 174 (top), 175 (top)

Westways Magazine (Automobile Club of Southern California), 103 (bottom)

About the Author

A professor of English at San Diego State College with a broad interest in history, George Sanderlin excels at writing books which combine historical source material with a spirited narrative.

First Around the World: A Journal of Magellan's Voyage; 1776: Journals of American Independence; Across the Ocean Sea: A Journal of Columbus's Voyage and *Benjamin Franklin: As Others Saw Him* are examples of his masterful and successful work in this genre, which gives the immediacy of the present to events of the past.

Mr. Sanderlin and his wife live near El Cajon, California.